As a pastor and teacher, I have
simple story to change lives. I'\
short stories that have meant someting --
them with others, and watched lives being changed for
the better. Some of my favorite stories come from
everyday family living.

I'm reminded of that when I think back to a time
when our daughter, Amy, now in college, was only five
years old. I had sustained a serious back injury while
playing racquetball. Unable to walk, I painfully crawled on
all fours. Our family and church were fervently praying for my recovery.
One Sunday morning, I was unable to preach or even attend worship services.
Amy, obviously frustrated over my situation, said to Debbie, "Mommy,
God's not trying very hard with Dad."

Amy put into words what most of us have thought or felt at some point in
our lives. "Where is God when I need Him?" we wonder. Or, "Why has He
abandoned me?" With Linda Delbridge, I have written this book to encourage
each of us to "keep looking up!" God does care! He does answer prayer! And,
He really does try very hard!

I offer this book as a way of saying "Thanks" to our Lord for giving me a
dad and mom who faithfully taught me by their words and actions to "keep
looking up!" As you experience the power of a short story, I hope that you will
also discover the healing power of a short prayer—

Lord, help me...
keep looking up!

John M. Palmer

"From my perspective, this is one of the most appealing and at the same time interesting formats I have ever seen. You have a best seller on your hands . . . Thank you for sharing this wonderful publication."

Charles T. Crabtree
Assistant General Superintendent
Assemblies of God

"The insights for daily living were delightful indeed— and so very practical . . . 'growth stuff' for everyday living. John has done a wonderful job in sharing with us all."

Pastor Fulton W. Butain
First Assembly of God Life Center
Tacoma, Washington

Stories to Keep You...Looking Up

Copyright 1999 by Landauer Corporation

Published by:
Landauer Books
A division of Landauer Corporation
12251 Maffitt Road, Cumming, Iowa 50061

President and Publisher: Jeramy Lanigan Landauer

Vice President: Becky Johnston

Managing Editor: Marlene Hemberger Heuertz

Art Director: Laurel Albright

Editor: Linda Delbridge, Ph.D.

Assistant Editor: Sarah L. Reid

Graphics Technician: Stewart Cott

Family portrait courtesy of Stover Photography

Library of Congress Cataloging-in-Publication Data
Palmer, John M. 1952-
    Stories to keep you—looking up: four seasons of wit & wisdom from / John M. Palmer;
    with Linda Delbridge.
        p.cm.
    ISBN 1-890621-00-5 (soft cover)
        1. Meditations. 2. Christian life—Assemblies of God authors. I. Delbridge, Linda. II. Title.

BV4832.2 P314 1999
242--dc21

99-047915

10 9 8 7 6 5 4 3 2 1

Stories to keep you...

Looking Up

Four Seasons of Wit & Wisdom from

JOHN M. PALMER

with
Linda Delbridge, Ph.D.

Left to right:
Jonathan, Amy, Bethany, Debbie, and John M. Palmer

Contents

To everything there is a season,
and a time to every purpose under heaven...

Ecclesiastes 3:1

A Season of Becoming

January
a time to be born

February
a time to love

March
a time to seek

Go confidently in the direction of your dreams!
Live the life you've imagined…for if you advance
confidently in the direction of your dreams,
and endeavor to live the life which you have imagined,
you will meet with success in common hours.

Henry David Thoreau

January
a time to be born

A few years ago, when I was only 33 years young, several members of the congregation where I still serve today remarked, "You're so young to be the pastor of such a great church." I'm grateful to God for this opportunity.

It made me reflect on how old does one really have to be to be an influence in the world?

Joash was 7 when he became king over Judah.
Joe Nuxhall was 15 when he joined the Cincinnati Reds as a starting pitcher.
Marcus Hooper was 12 when he swam the English Channel in 14 hours.
Cody Locke was 9 when he soloed his Cessna 150 near Mexico.
Benedict IX was 11 when he became Pope in 1032.
Joy Foster was 8 when she was the Jamaican singles table tennis champion.
Merril Wolf was 14 when he received his B.A. in Music from Yale.
David Brainerd was an early American missionary to the Indians who made an indelible mark before he died of tuberculosis at age 30.
Jesus was 12 when He astounded lawyers and doctors with His wisdom.

Lord, help me...
start young, think big, and never quit!

Ten Hut

To do what is right and just is more acceptable to the Lord than sacrifice.

Proverbs 21:3

General H. Norman Schwartzkopf has generated eleven rules for strong effective leadership.

1. Have specific goals and articulate them clearly.
2. Every morning, write down the five most important things to accomplish that day, and get those five done.
3. Let people know where they stand.
4. What's broken, fix now. Don't put it off. Problems that aren't dealt with lead to other problems.
5. No repainting of the flagpole. Make sure all the work your people do is essential to the organization.
6. Set high standards. People generally won't perform above your expectations, so it's important to expect a lot.
7. Lay out the concept, then let your people execute it.
8. People come to work to succeed. So don't operate on the principle that if they aren't watched and supervised they'll bungle the job.
9. Never lie. Ever.
10. When in charge, take command. The best policy is to decide, monitor the results, and change course as necessary.
11. Do what's right. The truth of the matter is that you always know the right thing to do. The hard part is doing it.

Lord, help me...
may my actions reflect my intentions.

There's a Way

"Where there's a will, there's a way." When our daughter Amy was in kindergarten, she helped me learn what that meant. It was a Friday afternoon in early January. I called home to speak with my wife Debbie. She had gone out for awhile and left Amy and her younger brother Jonathan with a babysitter. I left Amy a message to relay to her mother as soon as she arrived home.

So she wouldn't forget my message, Amy wrote herself a little note. When Debbie returned home, Amy promptly "read" the message to her Mom.

Since Amy hadn't learned to print yet, she used kindergarten shorthand to get the job done. On the note Amy had drawn a 5.30, a cross, and a figure similar to a snowman followed by what looked like a swirl of dust.

Amy told her mother, "Daddy will be home at 5:30. Call him at the office if there is an emergency." (Later I asked her why she drew a cross for "emergency." She replied, "I saw a cross one day on an ambulance.")

Because she was determined not to forget the message, Amy found a way to remember it. Where there's a will, there's a way—even when you're only in kindergarten!

The Courage to Continue

He wasn't well known outside Finland. He wasn't even considered to be among the top fifteen runners in the world in his event. But Lasse Viren had trained hard, and he believed he could win the 10,000-meter race at the '72 Olympics in Munich.

The seventy-five contestants had only run two and a half laps when one of the favorites collided with another runner and was thrown off the track. As he fell, he knocked Lasse to the track, head over heels. Lasse jumped to his feet and started running again, determined to catch up with the pack. Little by little, he gained ground. And to everyone's amazement, he crossed the finish line first and set an Olympic record.

Afterward, he summed up the race with this comment: "I found out I could be knocked down and still win." Lasse Viren is an inspiration in Finland today because he had the courage to get up after he had been knocked down.

Some of us have been knocked down by the rejection of a spouse, child, or parent. Others have been knocked down by news of a terminal illness, or by the unexpected and sudden loss of our job.

Still others of us have been knocked off the track after yielding to temptation. We can easily identify with this runner. It's painful to be knocked down, and very inconvenient. Our plans don't call for such unwelcome interruptions.

So what must we do? We need to draw courage from the Lord, just like Paul did at Lystra. (Acts 14:1–20) After stoning and dragging him outside the city, his enemies left him for dead. And to the surprise of many, but not of those who knew him well, he got up, went to the next town, and kept preaching.

Paul had the courage to continue! Later he wrote to his friends to encourage them. "We are hard pressed on every side, but not crushed; perplexed, but not in despair; persecuted, but not abandoned; struck down, but not destroyed." (II Corinthians 4:8, 9)

The Finnish fellow finished first! But that's not the most important. What truly matters is that he got up and kept running. Falls are only fatal when we give up!

We are hard pressed on every side, but not crushed; . . . struck down, but not destroyed.

II Corinthians 4:8, 9

Lord, help me...
when I've been knocked down, give me the courage to get up and finish what I started.

The Carpenter

In July 1987, Jimmy and Rosalynn Carter and scores of other volunteers gave tremendous time and energy to build fourteen Habitats for Humanity in Charlotte, North Carolina—in just one week!

In his book "The Excitement is Building," Habitat founder Millard Fuller relates his experience as he toured those new home sites. As he stopped briefly in front of one house, the young boy playing in the yard scampered toward Fuller's car.

"Hey," he said, "you got a pretty car."

"Yes, and you have a pretty house...What's your name?"

"D.J."

"Well, D.J., I want to ask you a question. Who built your new house?"

Millard expected him to say, "Jimmy Carter."

Instead, D.J. quietly replied, "Jesus."

Lord, help me...
credit the Master Builder for all He's done for me!

Winners

One of my favorite college basketball teams, the Drake University "Lady Bulldogs," lost a heart-breaker by one point in a conference tournament. I shared their disappointment and loss, but also wanted them to know they were still winners. So this is what I wrote for them—my definition of a "winner."

Winners realize that all of us miss the mark occasionally.

Winners love to win and hate to lose, but know how to do both graciously.

Winners know that the difference between winning and losing is determined by attitude, not the scoreboard.

Winners focus on the present and the future rather than dwelling on past victories or losses.

Winners don't criticize even if they feel justified in doing so.

Winners congratulate the opponent in loss or in victory.

Winners realize life consists of much more than outscoring someone else.

Winners aren't whiners.

Winners never give up, and they encourage others to do the same.

Winners always do their best even when the score shows them to be behind.

Let love and faithfulness never leave you. . .then you will win favor and a good name in the sight of God and man.

Proverbs 3:3, 4

God Sent a Professional

Just as the mother of a teenage boy slid a pie into the oven, the school nurse called and asked her to pick up her son and take him home because he was running a high fever. With the pie in the oven, the mom left immediately to get her son. By the time she arrived at school, the fever was worse and the nurse urged her to take him to their family doctor.

The mom drove to the clinic where the doctor examined her son, gave her a prescription for him, and told her to get him to bed right away. After taking the boy home, she headed for the mall and got the prescription filled. Hurrying to her car, she discovered that the keys were inside and the doors were locked.

She ran back to the mall, looking for a wire coat hanger. After finding one, she headed to the car when she stopped, stared at the coat hanger, and said to herself, "I don't even know what to do with this thing." She suddenly remembered the pie in the oven. Feeling frazzled and frayed, she began to cry as the frustrations of the past hour collapsed on her.

Standing on the curb the frustrated mom prayed, "Dear Lord, my boy is sick and needs this medicine. My pie is in the oven and my keys are locked in the car. And I don't know what to do with this coat hanger. Please send someone who knows how to use this. And I really need that person now, Lord."

Within seconds an old car pulled up to the curb and stopped in front of her. A young man with long stringy hair and ragged torn blue jeans got out of the car and walked toward her. As he passed by, she stepped out, held out the coat hanger, and asked, "Sir, do you know how to get into a locked car with this?"

Taking the hanger from her hand, he asked, "Where's the car?" He examined the door and window, deftly twisted the coat hanger, and just like that, the door was open.

The happy mom hugged him, exclaiming, "The Lord sent you. You must be a Christian."

The surprised young man stepped back and said, "No ma'am, I'm not a Christian. In fact, I just got out of prison yesterday for stealing cars."

She hugged him again, tightly. "Thank you, Lord," she cried. "You sent me a professional."

This is the confidence we have in approaching God: that if we ask anything according to his will, he hears us.

I John 5:14

Lord, help me...
have faith that You will answer prayer in
Your own time and Your own way.

Shooting at the Saints

If you keep on biting and devouring each other, watch out or you will be destroyed by each other.

Galatians 5:15

When the English and the French were at war in Colonial Canada, Admiral Phipps, in charge of the British Fleet, was ordered to anchor outside Quebec on the Saint Lawrence River. He was to await the coming of the British Infantry and then join his sea forces with the land forces to attack the French at Quebec.

Arriving early, Admiral Phipps, an ardent non-conformist, was annoyed by the statues of the saints that adorned the roof and the towers of the Catholic cathedrals of Quebec. So while waiting for his comrades to come by land, he ordered his troops to use the ship's guns to shoot at the saints atop the cathedral.

How many he hit, we don't know. But history recorded that when the infantry finally arrived and the signal for attack was given, the Admiral found himself without ammunition. He had used it all shooting at the saints.

Lord, help me...
put my energy into helping, not hurting others.

Playing it Safe

Many years ago in a Midwestern town, a lady lived and died. She was an elderly spinster, the oldest person in the town when she died. Although she had lived there all her life, she was not well known by the townspeople. She had done nothing seriously wrong, nor had she done anything of great note. When she passed away, the local newspaper editor wanted to report more than just the dates of her birth and death. He happened to stop by the local coffee shop where he learned that the proprietor of the tombstone shop was having a similar problem.

Even after thinking together about the problem, the two men were unable to arrive at a solution. The editor returned to his office and assigned the problem to the first person he found—the sports editor.

Today, if you were to visit the cemetery in that small town and find her tombstone, you would read this:

"Here lie the bones of Nancy Jones.
For her, life held no terrors.
She lived alone, she died alone.
No hits, no runs, no errors."

I have fought the good fight, I have finished the race, I have kept the faith.

II Timothy 4:7

Lord, help me...
make a difference in others' lives
by giving my best—mistakes and all!

Strategic Thinking

"Go," the Lord said to me, "and lead the people on their way..."

Deuteronomy 10:11

Reginald McDonough, who has served as Executive Director of the General Board of Virginia Baptists, defines leaders as "people who help others make the transition from the past to the future." He offers these guidelines of strategic thinking and action.

1. Focus on a vision of the future.
2. Learn all there is to know about the situation.
3. Concentrate on the big picture.
4. Look for breakthrough ideas.
5. Be willing to color outside the lines.
6. Be alert for patterns and cycles.
7. View change as an opportunity for growth.
8. Be willing to confront tradition.
9. Beware of the pooling of ignorance.
10. Give your ideas a reality check.

Lord, help me...
when You call me to lead others,
help me first follow You.

Yes, You Can

Early in his career, Henry Ford was ridiculed for trying to develop the automobile. Some of his best friends told him, "It can't be done."

One evening at a dinner, Ford was explaining his engine concept to those near him. Thomas Edison overheard the inventor and asked him to make a drawing.

When Ford had completed the crude sketch, Edison studied it intently, then banged his fist on the table. "Young man," he declared with confidence, "that's the thing! You have it. You can do it."

And Henry Ford did it!

Many years later, Mr. Ford recalled, "The thump of Edison's fist on the table meant the world to me."

... *"Everything is possible for him who believes."*

Mark 9:23

Lord, help me...
make my determination match my intentions.

Do It!

...for the Lord has chosen you to build...be strong and do the work.

I Chronicles 28:10

In the last few days of King David's life, he offered wise advice to his tenth son, Solomon, the heir-apparent to Israel's throne.

King David had good advice for this young man whom God had chosen to build the temple. David gave his son the building plans, the material provisions, and God's promises. The only thing Solomon had to do was build it. David's encouragement was simply, "Be strong and do the work."

What is it that you are to do? What challenge lies before you? What would you like to accomplish? Just do it! Many people die in obscurity having never achieved any great thing, only because they failed to take the first step. Often it is merely a fear of failure itself, which guarantees that nothing will ever be accomplished.

It's always better to do something imperfectly than to do nothing perfectly. Get started today—and just do it!

Lord, help me...
remember yesterday is a canceled check; tomorrow is a promissory note, and today is all I have to spend.

Seeing the Land

It was a fog-shrouded morning many years ago when a young woman named Florence Chadwick waded into the water off Catalina Island. She intended to swim the channel from the island to the California coast, a distance of about 26 miles.

Long-distance swimming was not new to Florence; she had been the first woman to swim the English Channel in both directions.

The water was numbing cold that day. The fog was so thick she could hardly see the boats in her party. Several times sharks had to be driven away with rifle fire. She swam more than 15 hours before she asked to be taken out of the water. Her trainer tried to encourage her to swim on since they were so close to land, but when Florence looked, all she saw was fog. So she quit—only one-half mile from her goal.

Later, she said, "I'm not excusing myself, but if I could have seen the land, I would have made it."

It wasn't the cold or fear or exhaustion that caused Florence Chadwick to fail. It was the fog.

Two months after her failure, Florence walked off the same beach into the same channel and swam the distance, setting a new speed record, because she could see the land!

Let us fix our eyes on Jesus, the author and perfector of our faith . . .

Hebrews 12:2

Lord, help me . . .
realize good vision makes possible great victories.

Nose Prints

...I have placed before you an open door...

Revelation 3:8

Some time ago, I was reminded again of how the Lord works with respect to "open doors." On a pastoral visit to a local hospital, I was entering through the E.R. door. It remained closed until I was just a few feet away, just close enough to trigger the mechanism which opened the door.

God often chooses to work like that in our lives. He has a perfect timing and very often the doors don't open until we are practically standing with our nose on the glass. This "faith living" requires patience, doesn't it?

Since we can't force a door to open, let's watch it open of its "own accord" in God's perfect time. If you're impatient, a final word of caution—don't press on the glass too hard with your nose. That hurts!

If we wholeheartedly trust the One with nail prints in His hands, we won't have to make nose prints on the door!

A Time for Reflection

It's here—the season for goal setting!

Regarding spiritual goals

- How much time each day will you commit to—reading the Bible... praying...memorizing Scripture?

- How much Scripture will you read this year—the entire Bible...once...twice?

- How much Scripture will you memorize—the New Testament...an entire book...two...a few chapters or verses?

- How will you carry out your own personal evangelism? To how many persons? Where will you find them? How will you go about it?

- How will you be an encourager? What is your plan for finding those who are discouraged? How will you put Christ's love into action?

- What form will your own ministry take this year?

A Time for Reflection

Within your family

- What do you want to have happen in your relationship with your spouse…your children?…your siblings…your parents?

- When will you have family worship? How often? How long? Who has what responsibilities?

How can you best improve or maintain your *physical health?* How do diet, exercise, rest, and weight control figure in? (Excuse the pun!)

Regarding mental or *self-improvement goals*, what topic areas, and skills will you focus on this year? How will you use tapes and books?

Professional goals might focus on skill development, increased productivity, greater creativity, improved team relationships, higher income, further training or education, looking for a job or finding a new career, etc.

In your *community* and neighborhood, how many of your neighbors do you plan to meet this year? What will you volunteer to do? Which children can you offer to take to Sunday school?

What are your *financial goals* in terms of income for this year? How much will you give in tithes, to missions, to other needs? How will you reduce debt? What kind of savings plan do you have in place?

Take a few minutes to write out your specific measurable goals for the New Year and plan to review them at the end of the year.

1. Spiritual goals:

2. Family goals:

3. Physical health goals:

4. Self-improvement goals:

5. Professional goals:

6. Community goals:

7. Financial goals:

He who works his land will have abundant food.

Proverbs 12:11

Doubt sees the obstacles; faith sees the way.
Doubt sees the darkest night; faith sees the day.
Doubt dreads to take a step; faith soars on high.
Doubt questions, "Who believes?"
Faith answers, "I."

February
a time to love

Some of the most tender times I experience with my children are just before bedtime, after our family prayers. Every evening that I'm home, when I tuck the children into bed, I usually say to each of them, "I love you and Jesus does, too."

On one such evening when Amy was in elementary school, she and I had a brief, yet very poignant exchange. I must share it because it reminds us that love is the giving of oneself—love is "being there."

On that particular Monday evening, she replied very sincerely, "Daddy, I know that you love me."

"How do you know I love you?" I asked.

"Because," she explained without hesitation, "you colored Easter eggs with me today and you ride bikes with me and you take every Monday off to be with us."

I hugged her! I smiled! I had a hard time falling asleep right away because I felt so good.

Lord, help me...
remember love is not buying big things;
love is being there for the little things!

# Love

An interlude in "You are Sixteen" from "The Sound of Music" underscores a basic principle of love—it's always in season!

"A bell is no bell 'till you ring it.
A song is no song 'till you sing it.
Love wasn't put in your heart there to stay—
Love isn't love 'till you give it away."

In I Corinthians 13: 4–8, 13, Saint Paul defined the love we are to give away.

Love is patient, love is kind. It does not envy, it does not boast, it is not proud. It is not rude, it is not self-seeking, it is not easily angered, it keeps no record of wrongs. Love does not delight in evil but rejoices with the truth. It always protects, always trusts, always hopes, always perseveres. Love never fails....

And now these three remain: faith, hope and love. But the greatest of these is love.

Lord, help me...
how much love have I given away today?

The Heart of Faith

Nicolas Berdyaev, who abandoned Marxism for Christianity, insists that neither history nor theology nor the church brought him to the Christian faith, but a simple woman known as Mother Maria.

Nicolas was present at a concentration camp when the Nazis were murdering Jews in gas chambers.

One distraught mother refused to part with her baby. When Maria saw that the officer was only interested in the correct numbers, without a word she pushed the mother aside and then quickly took her place.

This act of love revealed to Berdyaev the heart of Christianity—and the meaning of atonement. And that act of love led him to seek and follow Christ.

"The good shepherd lays down his life for the sheep."

John 10:11b

Lord, help me...
always thank You for giving
Your life for my life.

Love Changed Teddy's Life

Miss Thompson was a conscientious teacher who tried to treat all her students the same. However, one little boy was difficult for even Miss Thompson to like. His name was Teddy Stallard. Teddy didn't seem to be interested in school. He was not an attractive child, his schoolwork was horrendous, and his attitude was no better. In short, there was certainly nothing lovable about Teddy Stallard.

Indeed, for some strange reason, Miss Thompson felt a great deal of resentment toward Teddy. She almost enjoyed giving him "F's." Something about him just rubbed her the wrong way.

Miss Thompson knew Teddy's background. His school records indicated that in the first grade he showed some promise but he had problems at home. In the second grade, his mother became seriously ill and Teddy started falling behind. In the third grade, his mother died. Teddy was tagged as a slow learner. In the fourth grade, he was far behind. His teacher noted that his father had no interest in Teddy's progress. Miss Thompson knew Teddy's situation, but there was still something about him that she resented.

Christmas time came and the boys and girls in Miss Thompson's room brought her gifts. To her surprise, among those gifts was a very crudely wrapped present from Teddy.

Opening it in front of the other children, she discovered a gaudy rhinestone bracelet with half the stones missing, and a bottle of cheap

perfume. Sensing that the other children were beginning to smirk and giggle at the simple gift, Miss Thompson had the presence of mind to put on the bracelet and open the perfume. She put some on her wrist. She invited the children to enjoy her gifts.

"Isn't this bracelet beautiful?" she asked the children. "Doesn't this perfume smell lovely?" Taking their cue from her, the children quickly responded with "oohs" and "aahs."

At the end of the school day, little Teddy came to Miss Thompson's desk and said, "Miss Thompson...Miss Thompson, you smell just like my mother...and her bracelet looks real pretty on you, too. I'm glad you like my presents."

When Teddy left, Miss Thompson got down on her knees and asked God's forgiveness for her attitude toward Teddy. To make a long story short, from that day forward, Miss Thompson became a new teacher and Teddy Stallard became a new student. Both Teddy's attitude and his grades dramatically improved.

Many years later, Miss Thompson received a letter from Teddy telling her that he would be graduating from high school, second in his class. It was signed, "Love, Teddy Stallard."

Four years later, she received another letter from Teddy telling her that he was graduating from college, first in his class.

Four years later, yet another letter informed her that the young fellow who once presented her with a gaudy bracelet with half the rhinestones missing and a cheap bottle of perfume was now Theodore Stallard, M.D. Also, he was getting married. By now his father was dead, too. Would Miss Thompson be willing to sit where his mother would sit for the wedding if she were alive?

"You are all the family I have left now," wrote Teddy.

Miss Thompson sat proudly where Teddy's mother would have been seated at his wedding. That moment of sensitivity and compassion many years before had earned her that privilege and that joy.

Lord, help me...
reserve judgment until I've heaped on
a second helping of praise!

Care for My Son

A wealthy man died, apparently without leaving a will. Consequently, according to law, the estate was to be divided among the several surviving cousins who were the next of kin. Also as prescribed by law, the deceased person's household goods and other items of personal property were to be converted into cash at a public auction. During the sale, the auctioneer held up a framed photograph but no one bid on it, including the cousins.

Later, a woman approached the auctioneer and asked him if she might purchase the picture for a dollar, which was all she had. She explained that the photograph was a likeness of the deceased man's only son. She went on to relate that she had been a family servant when the boy lost his life trying to rescue a drowning person, and that she had loved him very much.

The auctioneer accepted the dollar and the woman went home and placed the photograph on a table beside her bed. It was then that she noticed a bulge in the back of the frame. She undid the backing and, to her amazement, found the rich man's will. The instructions in it were simple: "I hereby give and bequeath all my possessions to the person who cares enough for my only son to cherish this photograph."

Lord, help me...
to know You, because to know You is to love you.

...Jesus is the Christ...and everyone who loves the father loves his child as well.

1 John 5:1

The Compassionate Prince

After the First World War, the Prince of Wales was invited to visit a military hospital in which 36 injured soldiers were convalescing. He willingly accepted. In the first ward, he went from bed to bed thanking each soldier for his sacrifices for Great Britain and the Empire.

As the Prince left the ward, he spoke to the official in charge. "You told me there were 36 soldiers here, but I counted only 29. Where are the other seven?"

The official replied that the others were in very bad condition, and that they would never be able to leave the hospital due to their terrible wounds. "It would be better to leave them alone."

Undaunted, the Prince found the door and entered the ward. He proceeded to do just what he had done in the previous ward. As he left, he counted the number of soldiers. They totaled six.

Outside the ward, the Prince questioned the official again. "Where is the missing soldier?"

"Ah, Your Majesty, that soldier is in a little dark room by himself. He is blind, deaf, and completely paralyzed by the injuries he suffered. He awaits release by death."

The Prince of Wales quietly opened the door and entered the darkened room. He gazed with full heart upon the man lying helpless upon his bed. It was impossible to tell him of his concern, sympathy, and gratitude, for the man was profoundly deaf.

He couldn't communicate by shaking the man's hand, for he was paralyzed. He couldn't show the soldier how he felt, for he was blind.

In seeking some way to express himself, the Prince walked slowly to the bedside of the wounded soldier, and kissed him gently on the forehead.

...as God's chosen people... clothe yourselves with compassion, kindness, humility, gentleness, and patience.

Colossians 3:12

Lord, help me...
find a way to express Your love to everyone I meet today—
regardless of how difficult that may be!

Reach Up

Cast all your
anxiety on him
because he
cares for you.

I Peter 5:7

One evening when our Bethany was two, she and I headed upstairs after watching "Barney" and the evening news. She held a half-filled ten-ounce bag of potato chips. Realizing she couldn't carry the bag and walk up the stairs at the same time, she turned to me and with two words, handed over the bag. She simply said, "Help. Hebby."

I followed her up the stairs and carried the chips.

That is precisely what the Lord does for us—He takes our "hebby" loads and carries them for us. Your burden may not seem big to someone else, but if it feels heavy to you, God wants you to give it to Him. He loves it when you give Him your "hebby" heart!

Bethany's family knew what she meant even though she couldn't say all the words just right as a two-year-old. And God knows what we mean when we talk to Him from our hearts. It doesn't bother Him if we don't say everything exactly right. In fact, He even knows the meaning of our tears and our "sighs too deep for words."

Lord, help me...
ask for Your help when the load is "hebby."

Sticking Together

A sailor went fishing with a man who couldn't swim. It had been a dull and uneventful day until the man who couldn't swim hooked a really big fish—not the ordinary kind, but the kind that bends the pole and pulls the line taut, the stuff of dreams!

The man was so excited about snagging this big fish that he leaned over too far and fell into the water.

He began to yell, "Help! Help! Help! I can't swim! I can't swim!"

The sailor calmly reached out to pull the man to the boat by the hair of his head. But as he pulled, the man's toupee came off and the drowning man went under again.

When he came up, the sailor reached out again, and this time he got an arm. As he pulled on it, it too came off, because it was artificial. The man went under again, continuing to kick and thrash. The sailor reached out again, grabbed a leg, but as he pulled it, it came off as well. It was a prosthesis.

The man continued splashing, sputtering, and screaming "Help! Help!"

In frustration, the sailor yelled back, "How can I help you if you won't stick together?"

. . . you are the body of Christ, and each one of you is a part of it.

I Corinthians 12:27

Giving Everything

. . .in your
hearts set
apart Christ
as Lord.

1 Peter 3:15a

The mother of a family was celebrating her birthday and the other members of the family were treating her to a party. When the time came to give her gifts, she was instructed to sit in her favorite living room chair.

One by one, the father and the two older children came in from the kitchen, solemnly presenting her gifts on a silver tray as though she were royalty.

The smallest girl who had been left out of the gift selection process had been watching. After the others had given their gifts, she went into the kitchen, got the empty tray, placed it on the floor before her mother, stepped onto the tray, and said, "Mommy, I give you me."

The Spirit calls us to give ourselves completely and unconditionally to the Lord, not just now, but forever.

Lord, help me...
bring You my finest gift. Lord, I give You me.

Mister, Are You God?

Shortly after World War II came to a close, Europe began picking up the pieces. Much of the Old Country had been ravaged by war and was in ruins. Perhaps the saddest sight of all was that of little orphaned children starving in the streets of those war-torn cities.

Early one chilly morning, an American soldier made his way back to the barracks in London. As he turned the corner in his jeep, he spotted a little boy with his nose pressed to the window of a pastry shop. Inside, the cook kneaded dough for a fresh batch of doughnuts. The hungry boy stared in silence, watching every move. The soldier pulled his jeep to the curb, stopped, got out, and walked quietly to where the little fellow stood.

Through the steamed-up window, he saw the sumptuous morsels pulled from the oven, piping hot. The boy salivated and released a slight groan as he watched the cook place them ever so carefully onto the glass-enclosed counter.

The soldier's heart went out to the nameless orphan as he stood beside him. "Son, would you like some of those doughnuts?"

The boy was startled. "Oh, yes…I would."

The American stepped inside and bought a dozen, put them in a bag, and walked back to where the lad stood in the foggy cold of the London morning. He smiled, held out the bag, and said simply, "Here you are."

As he turned to walk away, the soldier felt a tug on his coat. He looked back as the child asked quietly, "Mister, are you God?"

Being His Hands

I lift up my
hands to your
commands...

Psalm 119:48a

In the courtyard of a small quaint church in a French village stood a marble statue of Jesus with His hands outstretched.

During World War II, a bomb fell too close to the statue and dismembered it. After the battle, citizens of the community decided to rebuild the statue they loved.

Even with its cracks and scars, the rebuilt statue looked beautiful to them. However, when they were unsuccessful in finding the pieces for the hands, some lamented, "But we can't have a Christ without hands!"

Someone else had another idea, and that perspective prevailed. If we were to visit that small French village today, we would see that same rebuilt marble statue of Jesus with arms extended, with no hands, and with a brass plaque on the bottom which simply reads, "Christ has no hands but your hands."

Lord, help me...
as I offer You my hands, let them move
at the impulse of Your love.

The Perfect Cure

February is best remembered for Valentine's Day. But every day is always a great opportunity to share some special moments, memories, and/or messages with the people you love so much. The following bit of prose made me smile because it is so true.

HUGGING—THE PERFECT CURE FOR WHAT AILS YOU

No movable parts
No batteries to wear out
No periodic checkups
Low energy consumption
High energy yields
Inflation proof
No monthly payments
No insurance requirement
Theft-proof
Non-taxable
Non-polluting
And, of course, fully returnable!

HUGGING IS HEALTHY

It relieves tension
It combats depression
It reduces stress
It improves blood circulation
It invigorates
It rejuvenates
It elevates self-esteem
It has no unpleasant side effects
It works miracles!

March
a time to seek

Seeking requires leadership, sometimes our own and sometimes that of others. How do we recognize leaders? When their priorities are packaged with productive problem-solving, creativity, generosity, vision, inspiration, and self-control as well as positive attitudes of affirmation and excellence. Most of all, leaders find solutions.

Perhaps the importance of focused seeking is exemplified in the story of a student who picked up the final exam for his European history class. The paper contained only one essay question intended to take the entire test period to answer. The essay question read, "Why did the Roman Empire fall?"

While others scribbled furiously, this particular student thought for a few minutes, wrote only a single word on his paper, and handed it in. His one-word answer? "Carelessness."

Lord, help me...
remember You're the short
answer for any serious problem!

No News is Good News

"I have told you these things so that in me you may have peace."

John 16:33

In June 1986, Amy and I were watching the 10:00 p.m. news. She was eager to hear the weather report because we had plans for outdoor activities the following day. After about twelve minutes of "news" (a murder, a strike, a serious accident, the farm crisis, and several other unpleasant happenings), the station broke for a commercial. Amy turned to me and asked hopefully, "Are the problems over yet?"— an interesting and accurate perspective from a five-year-old.

How often we find ourselves asking that same question, not always aloud, but to ourselves. Deep inside we are troubled, anxious, angry, and just plain tired of our trials and problems. With a sigh we ask, "Lord, are the problems over yet?"

The truth is, our days of testings, trials, and pressures are not over. Nor will they ever be over as long as we live here. But, "In Me," Jesus said, "You will have peace!" So cheer up! He has overcome the testings and trials. And since you are on His side, you will too!

True Leadership

Hundreds of years ago, Alexander the Great led a forced march across a hot and desolate plain. On the eleventh day, he and all the soldiers still with him were near death from thirst. Alexander pressed on.

At midday, two scouts brought him what little water they had been able to find—it hardly filled the bottom of a helmet. Their throats burning, Alexander's men stood back and watched him enviously.

Alexander didn't hesitate. He turned the helmet over and poured the water on the hot sand at his feet. Then he said, "It's of no use for one to drink when many thirst."

They desperately needed water—large quantities of it—when Alexander had but a few drops.

So he gave them the only thing he did have at the moment—inspiration. That's leadership.

Be devoted to one another in brotherly love. Honor one another above yourselves.

Romans 12:10

Lord, help me...
remember that what I do
speaks louder than what I say.

Better Now than Later!

But if we judged ourselves, we would not come under judgment.

I Corinthians II:3I

One Sunday a number of years ago, four-year-old Jonathan was having a bad day. He just couldn't seem to get in the flow of our family life that night. We tried humoring him, then kindly encouraged him to change his attitude, then warned him to "straighten up." Admittedly, it had been a long Sunday and he was tired. We were all a little frazzled and our "parental patience" was quickly wearing thin. He knew a spanking was imminent.

"Dad," he whispered in my ear, "I need to tell you something." I listened eagerly. "I'm going to go upstairs and get my pajamas on. And while I'm in my bedroom, I'm going to spank myself." What he did upstairs, I'm not sure. We heard no slap of his hand, nor was he crying when he came downstairs moments later. But he was smiling, cooperative, and happy the rest of the night.

Our son taught me yet another great lesson. By spanking himself, he avoided what would have undoubtedly been a harder and more painful discipline.

How much better it is if we can discipline ourselves!

Go ahead. No one's looking. Be spanked. Better you do it than Him! And better now than later!

Only the Captain Knows

An ancient story tells of a first mate on a sailing ship who wanted to become just like the captain, an imposing respected patriarch of the sea. Noticing that at certain times on the bridge the captain would unlock a private drawer, glance at something inside, then relock it before giving a command, the mate became convinced that the drawer contained the secret of nautical success.

One morning when the captain stepped away without locking up, the mate slipped over and peered inside. He saw a single piece of paper on which were written four words: Starboard—right. Port—left.

Your word is a lamp to my feet and a light for my path.

Psalm 119:105

Lord, help me...
make Your Word the secret of my success!

Digging Ditches

... *"Make this valley full of ditches... You will see neither wind nor rain, yet this valley will be filled with water, and you, your cattle and your other animals will drink."*

II Kings 3:16-18

When your life is characterized by turmoil, damaged relationships, painful trauma or loss, dig a ditch of forgiveness. Forgiveness is a two-sided coin that buys the freedom of two souls: yours and that of the person to be forgiven.

A college student by the name of Joe served on a fraternity initiation committee. The young men to be inducted had to stand the test. The older members took the initiates to a country road in the dark of night and forced them to stand in the middle of the road. Joe was given the job of driving a car at top speed toward the initiates until a member signaled the initiates to jump out of the way. Joe remembers driving down that dark country road and looking at the speedometer; it registered 100 miles an hour. Someone gave the signal and everybody jumped out of the way—except one person. He was killed instantly.

Joe spent time in jail. He had to leave college. His entire life was affected. He couldn't keep a job. He went from one job to the next and was inconsistent in his attendance and performance.

After he was fired from one particular place of employment, Joe was re-hired a few months later and returned as a totally different person. He showed up for work on time. He was kind to everybody and everyone loved him.

A colleague wanted to know, "Joe, what's the deal? You got fired from here a few months ago because you didn't show up at work and you were hard to get along with. Now everything is different. What happened?"

Joe shared this story. "After I left college, I went to jail. I got married and we had two children. I was difficult to get along with because every waking moment of my life, all I could see was that young man bouncing off the hood of my car. I was so filled with self-hate and anger and resentment, that eventually it drove me to drinking and I couldn't hold a job.

"One morning my wife was at work—it was her income that kept us together. When I answered a knock on the door, I found a woman who seemed strangely familiar to me. When she identified herself, I remembered. She was the mother of the boy I killed on that terrible night so many years before.

"She asked to come in. 'For years I have hated you. For years I have stayed up at night thinking of ways that I could get revenge against you. A few weeks ago, I asked Jesus Christ to come into my life, and He forgave me of all of my sins. I came to you today to tell you that I forgive you, and I ask if you will forgive me.'

"As I looked into her eyes, I saw love, and I knew that I could go on with my life again. In that moment, the love in her eyes told me it was okay.

"Her forgiving me let me go on with my life."

Keep Playing

Sing to him
[the Lord] a
new song; play
skillfully, and
shout for joy.

Psalm 33:3

A mother, wishing to encourage her young son's progress at the piano, took him to a Paderewski performance.

Upon arriving, they found their seats near the front of the concert hall. The boy couldn't take his eyes off the majestic Steinway on the stage.

While the mother visited with a friend, the boy slipped away unnoticed. Soon the spotlights came up and the audience quieted. Only then did she notice her boy sitting at the Steinway, playing "Twinkle, Twinkle, Little Star" like all beginners do, one note at a time. His mother gasped, embarrassed. Before she could retrieve her son, the master himself appeared on the stage and quickly moved to the keyboard.

He whispered to the boy, "Don't quit—keep playing." Leaning over, Paderewski reached down with his left hand and began filling in a bass part. His right arm reached around the boy, adding a running obligato. Together, the master and the novice held the crowd mesmerized.

Lord, help me...
no matter how simple my song,
let me keep playing it for You.

When Opportunity Knocks

I can do
everything
through him
who gives me
strength.

Philippians 4:13

Two shoe salesmen were sent to a far region of the South Sea. After they arrived, they went their separate ways. A few days later, the first sent back a message to the company saying, "Send me a ticket home. I don't want to stay. There's no future here. No one wears shoes."

A day later, the second salesman sent his report: "Send me 10,000 pairs. Everybody here needs shoes."

Both salesmen probably felt "a million miles away" from anyone or anything they knew. Both faced a challenge. But what a difference in how each responded!

One drew upon his creativity and broad vision; the other let psychological blindness and narrow-minded vision handicap him.

One was ready to give up and run away; the other anticipated a mission and great success right where he was.

Lord, help me...
turn big obstacles into even bigger opportunities!

Anticipating with Confidence

When we really listen to our children, we can learn a lot about them, us, God, faith, and life.

Children can teach us to believe. When Amy (now a college student) was three years old, she was saying her prayers before getting into bed. After praying for our family and friends, she prayed, "And, dear God, please give me a dog. "After a significant pause, she continued, "You will? Thank you! Amen."

Amy was anticipating that God would answer her prayer. That's the kind of faith all of us need. It is holy anticipation. It is being sure of what we hope for and certain of what we cannot yet see.

Lord, help me...
You will? Thank you! Amen.

Just Checking

In the days before most homes had their own telephones, a young boy walked into a pharmacy and asked permission to use the phone.

His side of the conversation went something like this: "Hello, Doctor? Do you need anybody to run errands for you, to mow your grass, shovel the sidewalk? Do you need anybody to work around the house?…Oh, you already have somebody?…Are you really happy with him?…You are really, really happy with him?…Okay."

He hung up the phone and started to walk out when the pharmacist said, "Son, are you looking for a job?"

"No, sir, I already have a job."

"But didn't I hear you talking to the doctor and asking him about mowing grass and running errands?"

"Yes, sir. I am that boy. I was just calling to check up on myself."

Lord, help me…
when I'm calling to check up on myself, to remember
the Great Physician has already written the prescription!

Scarred Hands

...I live by
faith in the
Son of God,
who loved
me and gave
himself for
me.

Galatians 2:20

A number of years ago before custody became so complicated, a young orphaned boy lived with his grandmother. One night their home caught fire. The grandmother tried to rescue the boy from his upstairs bedroom, but perished in the flames. No one in the crowd gathered outside knew what to do.

Suddenly a stranger rushed from the crowd and circled to the back of the house where he spotted a large iron pipe leading to the upstairs bedroom. He climbed the hot pipe, disappeared in the smoke, reappeared with the boy in his arms, and amid cheers from the crowd, climbed back down the pipe to safety.

Weeks later, a public hearing was held in the town hall to determine who would assume custody of the boy. Each person wanting the boy spoke briefly. A farmer stated, "I'd like to have him. Every boy needs to be in the outdoors, and I have a wonderful farm."

A teacher explained, "Every child needs to learn, and I've got a good library. I hope he lives with me."

A few others spoke, and then the town's wealthiest man stood. "I think he ought to come with me. I can give him a farm and a library, and anything he needs."

"Does anyone else wish to speak?" asked the person who was presiding.

From the back row, a stranger stood and walked to the front, his hands in his pockets. He stopped right in front of the little boy, who had stared at the floor throughout the meeting. Very slowly, the stranger removed his scarred hands from his pockets and held them for the boy to see.

With a cry of recognition, the boy lept to his feet, jumped into the arms of the stranger, and clung to his neck. There they stood: the stranger with his scarred hands and the little boy whom he had saved.

The room was quiet. The farmer stood and left. The teacher walked out. The wealthy man, too. The wounded man and the grateful loving little boy remained in their embrace. The man had won him, not with words, but with his life and actions.

There is in our midst One with scarred hands. His name is Jesus. It is our joyful response to leap to our feet and embrace Him, for the One with scarred hands gave His life on the cross so that you and I could have forgiveness of sins and eternal life.

Just as Jesus trusted His father, entrust your life to the man with the scarred hands.

Lord, help me...
be willing to do for others
what You have done for me already.

The Touch of Love

Sometimes the touch of love is more verbal than physical, as illustrated in this story from Sherman Rogers' book about logging in the Pacific Northwest.

As a young man, he worked in a logging camp, and on one occasion the boss needed to be away for some time and put Sherman in charge. "What exactly does that mean?" Sherman wanted to know. "Can I fire people?"

"Yes," answered the foreman, "and I know what you're getting at. You're going to fire Tony the first chance you get. I know he doesn't get along with anybody. He's nasty and he grumbles. But let me tell you something about Tony. He's been with me eight years. He's the first person to arrive on the job and the last to leave. Nobody has ever had an accident around Tony. His hill is always the safest to work on."

During the first day of his new responsibilities, Sherman arrived at Tony's hill and announced he had been put in charge. "I suppose that means you're going to fire me," challenged Tony.

"Actually, I was," replied Sherman, "but the boss told me you're the best workman we have. He said you're the first to come and the last to leave, and there's never been an accident around you."

Sherman was startled to see tears flowing down Tony's cheeks.

"Why didn't he tell me that eight years ago?" he cried.

Twelve years later, Tony was the head of one of the largest logging companies in the area. He never failed to remind Sherman that it all began on the day he was told what good things the boss had said about him.

Lord, help me...
offer words of encouragement sooner than later.

The Move Is On

"...As soon as you hear the sound of marching in the tops of the balsam trees, move quickly, because that will mean the Lord has gone out in front of you to strike the Philistine army."

II Sam. 5:24

Soon after David became king over Israel, the Philistines came against him. King David, asking God whether he should pursue them, received the unusual answer recorded in II Samuel 5:24.

As a boy, I remember singing this song in my home church, "The move is on, my Lord, the move is on...For I can hear the rustling in the mulberry trees, and I know, I know, I know, the move is on..."

I'm hearing those sounds! I'm confident God is preparing us. I'm fully convinced that God is calling us to move quickly. We are to take Jesus' love and power into every stratum of society.

It's beginning to rain. I hear noises. My faith is growing. God is leading. I am following. Please join me.

The move is on!

Seatbelts and Supplications

Sometimes we expect God to do things for us that we should be doing for ourselves. Someone has said it well, "When we do what we can, God will do what we can't!"

Years ago as I crossed through a downtown Des Moines intersection, an elderly person ran a red light and we collided. My car was smashed from the front door up, but I was unharmed. My seatbelt was buckled! I pray every day for protection for my family. I seek the ministry and intervention of angels daily, and they have done a great job. However, I must do my part.

Perhaps we need to be reminded...

...to pray for our children's salvation, but also to live a consistent, godly life before them.

...to pray for God's help financially, but also to use common sense in our spending habits.

...to pray for good health, but also to dress properly in cold weather, rest, and eat properly.

...to pray for spiritual strength to overcome temptation, but also to regularly feed our souls through prayer and the Word!

...to pray before taking a trip, but also to fasten the seat belt!

Jesus said to them, "My Father is always at his work to this very day, and I, too, am working."

John 5:17

A Season of Growth

April
a time to sow

May
a time to dance

June
a time to build up

If you have built castles in the air, your work
need not be lost; that is where they should be.
Now put foundations under them.

Henry David Thoreau

April
a time to sow

"I am only one, but I am one. I can't do everything, but I can do something. And because I can't do everything, I'll do the something I can!"

I was reminded of those encouraging words by Edmund Hale when I visited a town very few people had ever heard of, much less visited. Mitchell, South Dakota. A town on the South Dakota flatlands.

One with a small population, but a big desire—to let people know that "MITCHELL IS HERE." So they used what they had: a large building and lots of corn. They literally "sowed" the seed, and with a dream, some imagination, and determination, they have built the world's only Corn Palace. I saw it several years ago while speaking in the area. It's unbelievable. It's breathtaking!

The entire outside is decorated with thousands of bushels of native corn, grain, and grasses. The multi-colored scenes, which are changed every September, are of beautiful and intricate design. Not only has the Corn Palace given Mitchell a unique identity, but it has brought them millions of tourist dollars. The summer I visited, over 351,000 people toured this "Midwest wonder."

I tip my hat to residents of Mitchell, South Dakota! Instead of sitting around and complaining about the weather, or worrying about what they DIDN'T HAVE, they USED WHAT THEY HAD!

Only Then Could He Plant

Linda Delbridge learned about sowing from her father.

"Since he returned home from World War II, Dad has farmed his rich northwest Iowa loam, loving every inch of his dirt! For him, the cycle of the seasons began in late winter when he planned and prepared for spring planting. He checked the equipment, repaired and oiled, and then tried it out. He ordered the seed that best fit the growing conditions and the long-range forecast. He worked the ground, breaking up chunks of dirt and making the soil soft and receptive to the small seeds. Only then could he plant.

"Up and down the rows, he reflected on how this land had sustained his family since 1947, through sunshine and rain, through hail and drought, through early frosts and late springs, through corn borers and black nightshade. He marveled at how only God the Creator could make a small seed with the capability to send root and stem the right directions, with the great potential to reproduce itself thousands of times over.

"And every spring as he finished the final round, Dad climbed down from the tractor to stand on the land. 'I've tucked the seed in the earth, God, and now it's up to you to provide the sun and rain. Thanks for letting me do my small part one more year. Now I turn this year's crop over to you and ask you to bless it.'

"My father learned about sowing from the Master."

Four Steps to Your Dream

In the 1920's, a young African-American child in Cleveland was growing up in a home which he later described as "materially poor but spiritually rich."

One day a famous athlete, Charlie Paddock, visited school to speak to the students. At the time, Paddock was considered "the fastest human being alive." He told the children, "Listen! What do you want to be? You name it and then believe that God will help you to be it." That little boy decided that he, too, wanted to be the fastest human being on earth.

The boy went to his track coach and told him of his new dream. His coach advised him, "It's great to have a dream, but to attain your dream you must build a ladder to it. Here is the ladder to your dreams. The first rung is determination. And the second rung is dedication. The third is discipline. And the fourth rung is attitude."

As a result of that motivation, the young man won four gold medals in the Berlin Olympics. He broke the record in the 100-meter and in the 200-meter dashes. His broad jump record held for 24 years.

His name? Jesse Owens.

Lord, help me...
instead of staring up the steps,
help me to step up the stairs.

Coming Full Circle

Many years ago, the U. S. Army was building a highway in Alaska. They ran out of materials and therefore halted construction. Not wishing the crews to remain idle, the sergeant asked them to cut wood for the winter. Eager for a change in routine, they cut and piled wood with energy and speed. The crews worked feverishly at piling wood in long tall stacks along the highway.

A few weeks later, the sergeant discovered the construction delay would be much longer than anticipated, and the wood was piling up fast. Not wanting to cut more wood than necessary, he decided to find out what the winter would be like.

He heard that not too far away lived a local Alaskan Indian chief who was known to predict the weather with great accuracy. And so, donning his civilian clothes, the Army sergeant called on the Indian chief and asked him what the winter would be like.

The chief predicted a terribly hard cold winter.

"How do you know?" inquired the Army sergeant. "Is it because the leaves are turning early, or the birds are leaving early for the South, or is it because of the fur on the animals? How do you know for sure that we are going to have a terribly cold winter?"

"No, it's none of those things," the chief replied. "I can tell we are going to have a terribly cold winter because of the big heap of firewood the Army has piled up on the highway."

You Failed!

In 1985, when we moved from Athens, Ohio, to Des Moines, Iowa, there was one last item to take care of to make our move complete. I needed an Iowa driver's license. So I set out to get one.

I knew I would have to take a written examination, but I wasn't worried. In 16 years of school and college, I had never flunked a test. And furthermore, I reasoned, I'd been driving for 17 years and had a good driving record. And besides all of that, I have a good mind. I could figure out the answers.

I ignored my better judgement and did not study the book provided to me before the test. My test was graded. Then it happened: in that crowded driver's license room, the lady said loudly, so everyone could hear, "Well, Mr. Palmer, you've FAILED the test. You can take it again tomorrow. Would you like a book to study?" (I wasn't looking for a book; I was looking for a hole to crawl into!)

HUMILIATION! I learned a lesson again, "You reap what you sow." Had I not been over-confident and too busy to study, I could have passed easily. That night, I studied, and the next day, I passed with flying colors and obtained my Iowa driver's license.

I've been reflecting on what happened. I was reminded that someday I will take the ultimate test and I can only take it once. The result of that test is eternity, with or without the Lord. I'm taking no chances. I'm making preparations. I'm reading "The Manual" carefully. I'm trusting Christ, my Savior.

On that day I intend to hear my Lord declare (so everyone can hear), "Well, Mr. Palmer, you've PASSED the test!"

Some Things Never Change

A newly-wed husband was very surprised to find that his new bride followed a ritual when she fixed a roast. She always cut off part of the meat, then put the rest in a pan and prepared it. When he asked her about it, she simply said, "That's the way you're supposed to do it. That's the way my mother always did it."

The next week when invited over for Sunday dinner, he took the opportunity to ask his mother-in-law, "What's the right way to cook a roast?"

She explained, "You take the roast, cut part of it off, put the rest of it in the pan, and then cook it."

"How do you know that's the right way?"

"Because that's the way my mother did it!"

When the family gathered at Grandma's house for the next holiday, the confused newly-wed husband talked over the matter with her. "I understand that when you get a piece of meat, you cut off part of it and then put the rest in the pan and then prepare it."

"Oh yes," she nodded her head and smiled. "I did do that before I got a bigger pan."

Lord, help me...
realize that only when I'm willing
to change am I ready to grow.

Patience

Those who grow the Chinese bamboo tree have learned patience. When they plant, water, and fertilize it the first year, nothing happens. Not so much as a stalk comes out of the ground.

The second year, they fertilize and water it. The third year, they fertilize and water it. The fourth year the same, and the fifth. Not until the sixth year does it grow an inch.

And then in the sixth year, it grows fifteen feet within a matter of a few weeks.

If you've sown the seeds of compassion and friendship and watered them, wait patiently, for a bountiful harvest is certain. Don't give up—look up!

Let us not become weary in doing good, for at the proper time we will reap a harvest if we do not give up.

Galatians 6:9

Lord, help me...
keep on growing in Your love even if it doesn't show right away!

Rolls Royce Pride

Does protecting your reputation or pride prevent you from admitting your mistakes?

As an Englishman drove through the Swiss Alps at a rather high rate of speed, he broke the front spring on his Rolls Royce. He made it into the nearest town and called a nearby Rolls Royce center. After a company representative replaced the spring the following day, the Englishman was on his way.

When he got back to England, he had not received a bill for the spring and the service. He called Rolls Royce offices and asked that an accountant check the records for those services.

The accounts personnel insisted they had no such records. A few minutes later a very correct and stuffy Englishman, the Rolls Royce manager, was on the phone.

"There must be some mistake, sir," he said. "There is no such thing as a broken spring in a Rolls Royce. Therefore there can be no bill."

Lord, help me...
because You paid the bill,
I can admit my weaknesses.

A Lesson From the Links

If you've ever seen me golf, you know why no one ever asks me for tips on the sport. While I'm no pro, I have learned a few golf basics that serve me well as a follower of Christ, too.

1. Keep your knees bent. For the golfer, this provides good balance and a smooth swing. For the follower of Christ, "keeping your knees bent" is strong spiritual support. Jesus said that we should "always pray and not give up."

2. Keep your eyes on the ball. This is probably the most common error amateur golfers make. By lifting our heads while we swing, we can be assured we will "top the ball" or not hit it squarely. For the follower of Christ, "keeping your eyes on Jesus" will assure the ultimate victory.

3. Don't throw your clubs in the lake! Don't lose heart! Do your best, then quickly dispose of the scorecard. Keep your eyes on the goal; God will take care of keeping score.

Sow for yourselves righteousness, reap the fruit of unfailing love.

Hosea 10:12

Lord, help me...
swing like a pro at
the tasks You tee-up for me.

Getting Ready

With our daughter Amy's high school graduation approaching, we began working long and hard to get ready for the open house. Besides the food preparation for hundreds, we realized that we needed to do some repairs and sprucing up around the house. Since we hadn't done a thing with the landscaping in the front yard for the fourteen years we'd lived there, we decided to replace the lava rock and shriveled-up plants with new plantings and wood chips.

But that wasn't all! Because we planned to use the garage as a food-serving station, we decided to paint the walls, the ceiling, and the floor. Then there's the part of the yard that needed some sod. God provided the sod—free! The day before we were to lay the sod, I was doing my early-morning prayer walk and for some reason felt moved to walk and pray in a different part of the neighborhood. As I did, a sign on the fence caught my eye. It read: "Free sod—help yourself!" We did. And there was just enough for what we needed.

There's more...windows needed to be washed, shrubs trimmed, and the yard edged. And while we're at it, why not hose down the siding. Doing that, I noticed several sections of the siding were pulling away from the house. A little repair there...Better fix the basketball hoop, too.

Then it dawned on me that Jesus is getting ready for a huge open house. Trusting Jesus as my Savior means I'm ready and waiting for heaven's open house. I trust you are, too.

I Must Go!

Some years ago, a ship wrecked off the coast of the Pacific Northwest. A crowd of fishermen in a nearby village gathered to watch the ship as it smashed on the rocks. They sent a lifeboat to the rescue, and after a terrific struggle, the rescuers came back with all of the shipwrecked sailors but one. "The lifeboat was full; we had no room. So we told him to stay by the ship and someone would come back for him," one of the rescuers explained.

"Who will come with me?" shouted a young man from the gathering crowd.

Just then a small, fragile elderly lady cried out, "Don't go, Jim, my boy. Don't go. You are all I have left. Your father was drowned in the sea; your brother William sailed away and we've never heard from him; and now if you are lost, I'll be left alone. Oh, Jim, please don't go."

Jim listened patiently to his mother's pleading. "Mother," he spoke gently as he looked into her eyes, "I must go. It's my duty."

The onlookers watched as the men in the lifeboat fought their way toward the wreck. Anxiously, Jim's mother wept and prayed. The boat started back, a frail little shell tossed about by the angry waves.

At last it came within shouting distance, and the villagers called out, "Did you get him?" And Jim hollered back, "Yes, and tell Mother—it's William."

"Act with courage . . ."

II Chronicles 19:11b

Wisdom at Work

God gave
Solomon wisdom
and very great
insight.

I Kings 4:29

A good example of wisdom—the practical application of knowledge—is exemplified by the great inventor Thomas Alva Edison. He took special pleasure in showing guests around the grounds of his New Jersey home. On the way back to the house, the visitors had to pass one-at-a-time through a fence with a narrow opening and a turnstile.

"Why the turnstile?" visitors often asked.

"Each time you pass through," Edison would explain, "you pump eight gallons of water into a tank. We use that water for bathing and drinking."

Lord, help me...
grant me wisdom that comes from You,
I can do twice as much for Your kingdom.

Priorities

The phone in my office rarely rings at 6:30 on Saturday mornings. But it did one Saturday several years ago! The caller wasn't homeless, needing shelter and food. Nor was the caller requesting prayer or seeking information about our church. This caller was a young man, twelve years old who also happened to be our son, Jonathan.

He called with this question: "Is the gym at the church open at 7:00 this morning?

"I'm not sure if it is," I answered. "Why do you ask?"

"Because," he explained, "Our basketball game begins at 8:00 this morning and I've asked Mom to bring me in at 7:00 so I can shoot around and get warmed up for the game." Sure enough, at just a few minutes past seven, Jonathan was in my office, lacing up his basketball shoes, and heading to the gymnasium to get ready for the game.

On a normal Saturday, it takes a lot to get Jonathan out of bed. And on school days when we awaken him, he's a tad grumpy. Not so, however, when he has an early morning basketball game. He is cheerful and has boundless energy.

Our attitude helps determine our energy level. And our attitude is influenced by our priorities.

So, while I'm pleased that Jonathan enjoys basketball, I must admit I'm looking forward to the day when he calls at 6:30 a.m. on a Saturday to say, "I'm studying, Dad, and I have a few questions. Do you have time to help me?"

But seek first his [God's] kingdom and his righteousness, and all these things will be given to you as well.

Matthew 6:33

79

May
a time to dance

She wasn't singing in the rain, but she was singing in the shower—and quite early in the morning. I listened intently as Amy's singing punctuated the quietness: "Here am I," she sincerely sang, "send me to the nations as an ambassador for you…" I was moved as she sang it again and again.

Imagine my joy! Our eleven-year-old daughter, a fifth grader, getting ready to go to school, with a prayer song on her heart, "Here am I…"

It was hard to concentrate on my Bible reading as I thanked God for what I had just heard. Then about an hour later, I heard her again. While waiting for the bus, she was singing again, this time to her six-month-old sister, Bethany. An old hymn this time—"He took my sins away, He took my sins away, and keeps me singing every day. I'm so glad he took my sins away, He took my sins away."

She learned those songs in our Sunday evening services and our family evening devotions.

Our children are going to learn songs. And they are going to sing. The question is, what kind of songs will they sing?

"Sing to the Lord" wrote the Psalmist. It's a mighty good way to help keep your children close to God!

A Grad and Her Dad

Praise the Lord, O my soul, and forget not all his benefits...

Psalm 103:2

While prayer-walking this morning, I was praising God for His many blessings, including friendships and family. With deep gratitude, I prayed.

In the last two weeks, I've enjoyed observing Bethany learn to roller blade, watching Jonathan persevere in mowing the grass on a 90-degree day, and sharing in Amy's graduation from high school on May 30.

Honestly, I wasn't prepared for the flood of emotions I felt that day. It has been a joy to watch and help Amy grow. I remember something she said when she was just five years old. As she was painting Christmas tree ornaments, the paint was everywhere, including on her clothes. While trying to to get her cleaned up, Debbie said, "It's hard to be five years old." Later that day, during dinner, Amy spilled lasagna on her clothes. This time it was I who casually remarked, "It's hard being five years old, isn't it?"

Amy's reply was simple and accurate: "But you have to be five before you can be six." She was right. Messy clothes and spilled food are part of the growing-up process.

The six turned into seven, then into eight, nine, ten, and…now she's eighteen and standing in cap and gown with her graduating class. She will be leaving home for college in less than eighty days.

My heart swelled with pride and joy as I heard her name, "Amy Elizabeth Palmer," and watched her receive a diploma, with highest honors. The tears were happy tears.

At her Baccalaureate service there was a big lump in my throat as Amy introduced me to speak, saying, "Our speaker today is someone you may know. To many he's a pastor, to some he's a friend. To others he's a client or a consumer, but to me, he's a dad and a hero. He's a hero because he has lived a life worth imitating, a life of integrity. It is my pleasure to introduce to you the most important man in my life, John Palmer." Then she hugged me. The emotions were raging: more tears (bigger lump in the throat); joy (because she's grown up); sad (because I wish we had her a couple more years); joy (because she loves her Lord and her family; sad (because she'll be leaving for college in two months).

After sharing my heart with the seniors, encouraging them to always walk with God, and never give up, I sat down next to Debbie as Amy and seven of her friends sang, "This day is fragile. Soon it will end. And once it has vanished, it will not come again. So let us love with a love pure and strong, before this day is gone…This day is frail, it will pass by. So before it's too late to recapture the time, let us share love. Let us share God. Before this day is gone…"

A dad's dream! There, in our public high school, my daughter and her friends were encouraging their classmates to share love and share God. That's why this morning I prayed, "Thank you, Lord, for the privilege of being a dad."

Small—But Mighty

Little things can have a powerful impact on big things as evidenced by an unusual experiment conducted in a gun factory a number of years ago. A bottle cork, weighing less than four grams, was suspended by a silk thread alongside a heavy steel bar, which was hanging vertically from a beam by a slender metal chain.

The cork was set in motion and it began to swing gently against the heavy steel bar. At first nothing seemed to happen. The cork continued to swing back and forth against the motionless steel bar.

Then, the steel bar started to tremble, and a few moments later, it shuddered. The cork didn't stop. Steadily it continued its assault on the heavy steel bar. Soon, the movement of the great steel bar took up an orderly pattern of motion.

Eventually, the massive steel bar picked up the rhythm of the tiny swinging cork.

In another half hour, the cork was taken down, but the steel bar continued to swing back and forth as rhythmically and steadily as a clock pendulum.

Lord, help me...
have the courage to be a small cork
in a steel-beamed world.

Leading by Example

The story is told of a dean of a small college in Pennsylvania who was informed that the walls of a certain men's dormitory were smeared with shaving cream, peanut butter, and jelly. He went over to investigate. Of course, not a soul around had any idea how it could possibly have happened. In room after room, he met with surprised innocence.

The dean had several options. He could make every man in the dormitory go to work and clean it up. He could call the custodian. There was a third option.

Leading by example, he got a bucket and a brush and set to work cleaning the walls. One by one, doors opened, heads popped out, word spread of what the dean of the college was doing. Soon, he was not alone in the scrub job.

...whoever wants to become great among you must be your servant...

Mark 10:43

Lord, help me...
remember that the greatest leaders
are often the greatest servants.

Make a Joyful Noise

I will extol the Lord at all times; his praise will always be on my lips.

Psalm 34:1

Evangelist C. M. Ward was a powerful, colorful preacher. I was blessed to have him as a ministry mentor during my years at Central Bible College. He loved to tell this story.

In 1865, with a song book under his arm and a vision in his heart, William Booth, the Methodist preacher who founded the Salvation Army, went to the saloons and pubs of the east side of London and began to preach. People threw rotten eggs and tomatoes at him, but he kept on preaching. At the end of the sermon, he invited them to give their hearts and lives to Jesus Christ. A number accepted that invitation. One by one, the drunkards, the gamblers, and the prostitutes turned their lives around, as God's power transformed them.

Soon they began to sing up and down the streets of east London. Before long, singing wasn't enough. Even though they owned none, they wanted to play instruments. When a London ship band went out of business, the converts purchased all the instruments. They weren't musicians and they had no teachers or lessons, but by trial and error, these men and women learned that if you blow in here and press this here, certain sounds will come out.

They went into the streets of London and played their instruments—and were hit with eggs and tomatoes. People scorned them and laughed at them, but they kept playing.

That was the beginning of the Salvation Army band.

They got so excited about their instruments that they decided to enter a music contest and compete with highly trained musicians. The judges were masters in the field, including the famed Doctor Farmer. When Doctor Farmer listened to them play, his old British heart went out to them. He knew he had to help them. He first advised the bass drummer, "I appreciate your effort and your enthusiasm, but you can beat the drum a little less violently. Use a little more wrist action."

"Doctor, I know I'm not a good drummer," the man replied. "Less than eighteen months ago, I was a hopeless drunkard. There wasn't a stick of furniture in my house. There wasn't even bread for my children. Jesus changed all that and I'm sober now. The living Christ has turned my booze into bread and my liquor into furniture. And when I begin to think of what Jesus has done for me, I get so happy I could bust the blessed thing."

Doctor Farmer approached the French horn player next. "You know, I appreciate your willingness to tackle one of the most difficult instruments, the French horn. But you're blowing too hard. It's got to be played more delicately. Put your lips to the mouthpiece softly and just sort of kiss it."

The man laid the horn down, smiled, and said, "Doctor, let me tell you what happened to me. A few short months ago, I was an enslaved gambler. I could sit for hours at a gambling table without food or sleep. My family was separated. I was alone. One day, Mr. Booth was preaching and I accepted Jesus Christ, and He's come into my life. He saved me and totally changed me, and He's restored my loved ones to me. When I start thinking about what Jesus has done for me, I could blow that blessed thing straight out."

Different Dreams

Two young medical students at the University of Michigan had just finished their classes in the spring of 1883. As they relaxed in their rooms, their thoughts focused on what they would do with their lives.

The two differed markedly in appearance: the one short and stocky, the other tall and thin with blue eyes.

"Come on, Will," the short one urged. "Come to New York with me. We'll make a great team. All sorts of wealthy people live back East—we'll be rich in no time at all. What do you say?"

This multi-month continuous discussion had centered around the dream of going East and setting up a partnership in New York City.

"I'm sorry, Ben," the other young man replied, "but the more I think about it...well, I'd like to practice with you, but...".

"Will, you're a fool!" the other countered. "The Midwest is a cheap place to study medicine, but no place to practice it—nothing but small towns and farmers, none of them with any money. You'll never make a dime out here."

"You're probably right, Ben."

"Well, then, come East with me. We'll travel in Europe, hobnob with all the greats of the world. We'll meet beautiful rich young women. With our talent, we can't miss!" the other persisted.

Will remained silent for a moment, then confessed, "It's a tempting picture you paint, Ben. But it's just not what I want. I want first of all to be a great surgeon—the very best, if I have the ability..."

The other interrupted, "And you will be. What's wrong with getting rich in the process?"

"Nothing, I suppose. But what about these people here? They need good doctors, too—even if they can't always pay. No, I think I should go back home to Minnesota and give them all the help I can."

Some weeks later they parted—Ben going to New York with his dream of getting rich by treating the wealthy and powerful of the city. Will headed for Minnesota where he became a horse-and-buggy surgeon, helping his father, a general practitioner. The two of them ministered to the sick in the small towns and farms in and around Rochester.

In the years that followed, nothing much was heard of the ambitious young doctor with his dream of getting rich in New York City.

As for young Will, he and his younger brother Charles grew the Mayo Clinic from a smaller clinic founded by their father in 1889 in Rochester. Eventually, Will Mayo did treat the wealthy and powerful from the East and from around the world, just as his college friend had wanted.

But he did not go to New York. Instead, they came to him in Rochester, Minnesota.

"I will give you a wise and discerning heart . . ."

I Kings 3:12

I Love Storms!

Three-year-olds can teach us some pretty powerful lessons. To celebrate Amy's and Jonathan's completion of seventh and first grade respectively, we decided to go out for dinner. By the time Jonathan's little league game was over, it was raining "cats and dogs," and the lightening was brightening the sky like fireworks on the Fourth of July.

We went to Johnston's Hardee's for their fried chicken special. When we walked inside, we were surprised to find that we were the only customers in the store. While ordering our meal, the lights went out! A battery-operated generator turned on, providing one small light in the middle of the restaurant seating area. I would have preferred to take the food home to eat, but the children were excited to eat in the dark. They won.

Bethany was more interested in her two dolls and baby stroller than the chicken dinner. Sitting alone in the middle of the floor, she talked to her dolls. Since we were the only ones in the restaurant, we didn't figure she was bothering anyone, so we let her play. It was then that I heard her say to her dolls, "Hallelujah, I love storms!"

What struck me most was not just what she said, but how she said it. She was so calm and relaxed, unaware of the potential dangers of lightening: falling trees, fires, and power outages. She evidently felt very secure, perhaps because her whole family was together.

I've been reflecting on those words, "Hallelujah, I love storms!" Frankly, I don't care for storms and tests. I'm trying to remember the last trial I went through in which I confessed, "Hallelujah, I love storms!"

While I kept a fairly positive attitude during a siege with my back, no one heard me lying on my bed, unable to walk and work, saying "Praise God, I love this storm!"

St. James gave good advice when he encouraged us to let our patience grow, and don't try to squirm out of our problems. In other words, stop whining and start blessing!

Consider it pure joy . . . whenever you face trials of many kinds . . .

James 1:2

Lord, help me . . .
stop squirming and start singing!

The Choice is Yours

For some people, serving the Lord is a JOB. For others, it is a MINISTRY. What's the difference?

If you are doing it just because no one else will, it's a job. If you are doing it to serve the Lord, it is ministry.

If you are doing it just well enough to get by, it's a job. If you are doing it to the best of your ability, it is ministry.

If you quit because someone criticized you, it was a job. If you keep on serving, it is ministry.

If you'll do it only so long as it doesn't interfere with your other activities, it's a job. If you're committed to staying with it even when it means letting go of other things, it is ministry.

If you quit because no one ever praised you or thanked you, it was a job. If you stay with it even though no one notices your effort, it is ministry.

It's hard to get excited about a job. It's almost impossible not to be excited about a ministry.

An average person does a job. A great and growing person is involved in a ministry.

If your concern is success, it's a job. If your concern is faithfulness, it is ministry.

People will say, "Well done," when you do your job.

The Lord will say, "Well done, good and faithful servant" when you complete your ministry here on earth.

A Willing Servant?

Many people sincerely say they want to serve the Lord—but often it is on their own terms and conditions. One such person wrote this letter.

Dear Lord,

I want to serve You so badly! I'm literally burning with the fever. I've been on vacation and I'm more ready than ever to find a special ministry. What I need now is an assignment. That is what I want to discuss with You.

I've been asked to serve as program chairperson for the women's group, but I'm hoping You will agree with me that this isn't quite the right job for me. The Junior Department of the Sunday School needs a teacher badly, but I know too many of the children—wild bunch, difficult to control, not much fun. (Actually, it's no wonder they're so awful, considering the homes they come from.) I would love to help in the nursery, but that would mean missing the service occasionally, and I know You wouldn't want me to do that. Besides, my children are too old for the nursery so I'm sure no one expects me to work there now. The woman next door can't drive, she needs help with the groceries, and needs company; but she's such a trial—she never lets you go once she gets hold of you.

How about something different? NO nursing homes, please. It just breaks my heart to see the mental and physical problems the elderly endure. I know You will think of something. I can hardly wait! I am so happy when I can minister in Your name.

With all my love,
Ima Servant

The Power of a Seed!

A Paul Harvey story tells of the dormant power of a seed. Workmen in a Kemigawa farmyard twenty-five miles southeast of Tokyo were digging in a peat bog when they made an incredible discovery. They called in the experts who investigated what lay inside the fossilized remains of a canoe eighteen feet under the ground.

We do not know the details of how their find was removed to the safety of a laboratory. We only know that it got there. We also know that Dr. Ohga kept a round-the-clock vigil, and that in four days, under laboratory-created climate conditions, they found perceptible movement!

Cameramen were summoned to record this unprecedented resurrection. Japan's scientific community was alerted to the surprise that there was life left over from the time when Roman legions first invaded England. A living thing had survived from prehistoric Japan. The chain of unbroken links which comprised Oriental psychology, sociology, philosophy, and theosophy had led a living thing from the lifeless past to join them in the present.

For in a peat deposit, eighteen feet below the earth, cradled in the fossilized remains of a canoe, they had discovered a two-thousand-year-old ungerminated, dormant, apparently lifeless…SEED!

And after four days, a sprout; after fourteen months, a delicate pink lotus flower. The seed that went to sleep when Jesus did… was awake!

Mom is "Wow!"

I love Jacqueline McDermott's story.

She relates, "I have four daughters, and we all seem to wear the same size. To keep my laundry from disappearing, I started marking my underwear 'MOM.' One morning I found my dresser drawer empty. Going straight to the girls, I asked, 'Do any of you have underwear that says 'Mom' on it?'

"'No,' said Karen, my third daughter. 'All of mine say, WOW.'"

I'm convinced that my wife, Debbie, is a "WOW MOM." In one day alone, Debbie was the model of service to her brother and her daughter. Because her brother, Doug, was receiving a prestigious award from his alma mater, Debbie drove seven hundred miles round trip to Springfield, Missouri, to be with him as he was honored. Before Debbie left that morning, she asked eight-year-old Bethany if she'd like to make dinner for me that evening. Of course, Bethany was elated. Debbie showed her how to cook green beans and fry a piece of ham on the stove.

After school, Bethany called me at the office and announced, "Dad, I'm going to cook dinner for you tonight. It will be ready in thirty minutes." Sure enough, when I arrived home, dinner was ready.

While her older sister Amy was there to supervise, it was Bethany who made my dinner. And thanks to her WOW MOM, she was excited and happy to have such an important new job!

Debbie accomplished a lot in just one day!

Power to the People

...you are
a chosen
people...
a people
belonging to
God...

I Peter 2:9

The late Bishop G. Bromley Oxnam tells of giving the annual Memorial Day address at the National Monument at Gettysburg. Like many other speakers, he felt the need to conclude his speech by reciting Lincoln's famous address. After he finished, he felt all had gone well. That is, until an old, old man made his way forward and remarked, "Son you made an awful mess of Lincoln's speech."

Oxnam asked, "What do you mean? I didn't miss a word of it. Here, look at my notes."

The old man replied, "Oh, I don't need your notes, I know it by heart. You see, I heard it the first time around."

By now, Bishop Oxnam realized that this man had been present when Lincoln originally delivered his words. He was curious about how his recitation had differed from that of the President.

The old timer explained it this way. "Abe put his hands out over the people like a benediction and said, 'That the government of the people, by the people, and for the people should not perish from the earth.'

"You got the words right, son, but you missed the real message. You emphasized GOVERNMENT. Lincoln talked about PEOPLE."

Slow Me Down, Lord

"Slow me down, Lord. Ease the pounding of my heart by the quieting of my mind. Steady my hurried pace with a vision of the eternal reach of time. Give me amid the confusion of the day the calmness of the everlasting hills.

"Break the tensions of my nerves and muscles with the soothing music of the singing streams that live in my memory. Teach me the art of taking minute vacations, of slowing down to look at a flower, to chat with a friend, to pet a dog, to smile at a child, to read a few lines from a good book.

"Slow me down, Lord, and inspire me to send my roots deep into the soil of life's enduring values that I may grow toward my greater destiny. Remind me each day that the race is not always to the swift and that there is more to life than increasing its speed. Let me look upward to the towering oak tree and know that it grew well and that it grew straight and strong because it grew slowly and well.

"Slow me down, Lord."

". . . ask where the good way is, and walk in it . . . and you will find rest for your souls."

Jeremiah 6:16

Lord, help me...
when I need a speed limit!

An Encouraging Word

I am convinced that neither death nor life... neither the present nor the future... nor anything else in all creation, will be able to separate us from the love of God.

Romans 8:38, 39

June Nadle's co-worker was preparing for a funeral service and noticed that the florist had failed to place a ribbon with the words "Beloved Brother" on the casket spray.

An employee rushed to the flower shop, had the ribbon prepared, and hastily added it to the arrangement just as the family arrived for the funeral. After the memorial service, the sister of the deceased paused at the casket to pay her last respects and noticed the ribbon she had requested. To her horror, it read "Beloved Bother."

It can be very embarrassing when we get the message mixed up. Like the time the preacher told his large Sunday morning congregation, "I was informed earlier this morning that Bill Morris died yesterday." Then the pastor proceeded to pray fervently that God would comfort Bill's family. You can imagine the pastor's surprise, shock, and embarrassment when Bill met him at the door at the conclusion of the service and said, "Thanks for the encouraging word, Pastor."

Well, I haven't got the message mixed up, and I do have an encouraging word: God is on his throne and He will fulfill His plan and purpose in you!

Happy Pappy

Bethany, our youngest child, loves to tease. When she was four or five years old, she began teasing me by calling me "Silly Willy." I spontaneously responded, "I'm not 'Silly Willy,' I'm 'Happy Pappy.'" She still calls me "Silly Willy," while I say that I'm "Happy Pappy."

Because our children provide lots of smiles and happy memories, I really am "Happy Pappy," a glad dad! Recently after the Saturday evening service I went to my office and found two "sticky notes" on my desk. I smiled and nearly cried with joy as I read them: "Dear Dad, I hope you had a good day at work. I love you, Dad. Love, Bethany. "

The second note was a P. S.

"I will see you at home if you come before I to go sleep. Love you!"

I had planned to stay awhile longer and call recent visitors to invite them to worship with us again. But after reading that note, I went right home to spend time with Bethany before she went to sleep. Priorities!

"At that time I will gather you; at that time I will bring you home."

Zephaniah 3:20

Lord, help me...
make You a glad dad!

A Time for Reflection

A dancer cannot maintain balance by staring at his or her feet, but sustains equilibrium by finding a focal point some distance away. So also, we find joy in the dance and maintain our spiritual balance when we focus on someone beyond ourselves.

Just as a dancer must stay in good physical and mental condition to experience success, so also we must stay in good spiritual shape through prayer and the Word if we are to find soul support for dancing with joy.

The following warm-up list, adapted from Alfred A. Montapert's "Ten Steps to Brighten Your Life," suggests ways we might enter dances of joy. Read through the first nine steps and then add your own dance routines at the bottom of the page! Keep this list handy for those times you need to support your soul with a dance of joy!

1. Begin the day in a calm and cheerful mood. Know this is the day the Lord has made, and rejoice in it!

2. Smile at others. It's contagious and you will feel lifted up when smiles are redirected at you.

3. Count your blessings—one by one. Realize the real wealth you already have.

4. Be adventurous. Take a walk and see new neighborhoods, new buildings and parks, new scenery.

5. Call a friend or write a letter. Let a friend know he/she is in your thoughts and prayers. Offer a word of encouragement—it's oxygen for the soul.
6. Look for the bright side of life. Having a cheerful, loving attitude is good for your health!
7. Do a good deed or give something beneficial to a loved one.
8. Give of yourself. Offer your services to a hospital or church. Help people. The law of giving will reward you tenfold.
9. Do the best you can each day.
10. I can…
11. I will…

You will go out in joy and be led forth in peace…

Isaiah 55:12a

Lord, help me…
to find joy in the dance.

June
a time to build up

When the Son shines, He brings light and warmth, and He stimulates growth. After spring and summer showers saturate the ground in the Midwest, and the sun is in direct alignment with our part of the world, then the grass flourishes as sun and rain build it up.

Jesus said, "I am the vine; you are the branches. If a man remains in me and I in him, he will bear much fruit; apart from me you can do nothing." (John 15:5)

When we are connected to Jesus, He shines in our lives and builds us up as we grow through affliction, in balance, in compassion, in devotion, in eagerness to serve, in faith and faithfulness, in generosity and gentleness, in honesty, in integrity, in joy, in knowledge, in love, in meekness, in nurturing others, in obedience, in peace and patience, in quiet communion with the Lord, in resolve, in self-control, in tenderness, in usefulness, in virtue, in ways of serving Him, in "x-citement," in yieldedness, and we are built up zestfully in a zillion ways!

Lord, help me...
increase my zest quotient for today.

Teammates

*...encourage
one another
daily...*

Hebrews 3:13

One of my summer pleasures is playing on one of our church softball teams in the Clive city league. We have a lot of fun.

A couple of weeks ago, however, we had a tough game. We got pounded. The opposing batters were huge, the size of Division I football players. They crushed my pitches, hitting several home runs, while we scored just one run. One of their players, who weighed at least 230 pounds, hit a hard low line drive that caromed off of my left ankle and into right field.

Many days later my ankle was still swollen and my foot several shades of black and blue. It was, as you might guess, a game I'd love to forget.

As we were being thoroughly trounced, we continued to encourage each other. One of our best hitters, after making an out, came back to the bench and encouraged the next batter, saying, "Pick us up, T. K. Pick us up." Encouraging one another: That's what teammates do."

Lord, help me...
even when I'm down,
let me be "up" for others.

It's Not the Dough!

A. J. Cronin loved to tell of a taxi ride he once had in New York City. From the driver's non-verbal expressions and the way he slammed the car into gear, it was obvious to this great British physician and author that the driver was upset.

After some small talk, Cronin asked the taxi driver what was wrong. He replied, "I've got good reason to be sore. One of my riders left a wallet in my cab this morning with nearly three hundred dollars in it! I spent more than an hour trying to find the fellow. Finally when I found him at his hotel, he took the wallet from me without a word and glared at me as if I had snitched it."

"Did he give you a reward?" Cronin asked.

"Not a cent for my time or gas. But it wasn't the dough I wanted…" Then he exploded, "If the guy had only said something."

I've done the same sort of thing. I've failed to say a sincere "thank you" when it was obvious that one was needed, appropriate, and expected. The nine lepers whom Jesus healed did the same thing—only one of them returned to thank Him for healing them!

Why not take a little time in the next few days and write a few notes of appreciation to people who have made a significant impact in your life.

One of them, when he saw he was healed, came back…threw himself at Jesus' feet and thanked him…

Luke 17:15,16a

Picking Each Other Up

Over the years, while ministering in Montana, our family has taken several day trips into gorgeous Glacier National Park, visiting Logan's Pass, and hiking to Hidden Lake. The second time we were joined by Debbie's brother Doug and his family. Since Jonathan and Bethany are about the same ages as Ashley and Kaylee, having them along was extra special.

Early in the hike Bethany and Kaylee, the two youngest, led the way. As they marched boldly up the hill, they would turn around and encourage us, saying, "Let's pick up the pace."

But as we approached the middle portion of the long upward hike, they were tired and cold, and stopped often to rest. I encouraged them with Paul's words, "I can do everything through him [Christ] who gives me strength." (Philippians 4:13) They kept hiking.

At one point in the hike, the climbing was steep and the snow was very slippery. When the two girls' pace had slowed considerably, I said, "Over this next hill is a mama mountain goat and her babies."

With those words, the girls began running to the top of the hill with renewed energy. We did see the mountain goats and we made it to Hidden Lake, as we picked each other up.

Lord, help me...
when I'm down, send someone to pick
me up so I can return the favor!

Ringing the Bell

Did you hear the story about the time Arnold Palmer met a blind golfer? Palmer was not only amazed that the man could play, but that he was so good. "What's your secret?" Palmer asked.

The blind man explained, "I have my caddy stand at the hole and ring a bell. I just aim at the noise." Then he challenged Palmer to a match. The great pro, not wanting to humiliate the blind golfer, declined.

When the man said he'd play him for $10,000, Palmer changed his mind and asked, "When do we tee off?"

The blind golfer quickly replied, "Tonight, at 10:30."

Over the years, I've learned that no matter what our handicaps and challenges, we can accomplish a lot as long as we have someone to walk with us and ring the bell for us.

From him the whole body... builds itself up in love...

Ephesians 4:16

Lord, help me...
in the seasons of life, let me both hear the
bells and ring them for others.

Walt

*...be patient,
bearing with
one another
in love.*

Ephesians 4:2b

In their book, "As Iron Sharpens Iron: Building Character in a Mentoring Relationship," Howard and William Hendricks share the following story:

I can recall several influential figures who were strategically used by God to change the course of my life. The first was a man named Walt. Had it not been for Walt, I seriously doubt whether I would have ever become a follower of Jesus Christ.

I came from a broken home. My parents were separated before I was born, and neither one paid much attention to my spiritual condition. To put it bluntly, I could have lived, died, and gone to hell without anyone even bothering to care. But Walt cared. He was part of a tiny church in my neighborhood that developed a passion to affect its community for Christ.

Walt's passion was to reach nine- and ten-year-old boys like me with the gospel. I'll never forget the Saturday morning I met him. I was sprawled out on a Philadelphia sidewalk playing marbles. Suddenly someone was standing beside me. I looked up to see this gangly guy towering over me—all six feet, four inches of him. My mouth sort of dropped open.

"Son, how would you like to go to Sunday School?"

That was an unfortunate question. To my mind, anything that had the word "school" in it had to be bad news. So I shook my head no. But Walt was just getting started. "How would you like to play marbles?" he asked, squatting down.

Now he was talking my language!

"Sure!" I replied, and quickly set up the game. As the best marble player on the block, I felt confident that I could whip this challenger fairly easily.

Would you believe he beat me in every single game! In fact, he captured every marble I had. In the process, he captured my heart. I may have lost a game and a bit of pride that day, but I gained something infinitely more important—the friendship of a man who cared. A big man, an older man, a man who literally came down to my level by kneeling to play a game of marbles. From then on, wherever Walt was, that's where I wanted to be.

Walt built into my life over the next several years in a way that marked me forever. He used to take me and the other boys in his Sunday School class hiking. I'll never forget those times. He had a bad heart, and I'm sure we didn't do it any good, running him all over the woods the way we did. But he didn't seem to mind, because he cared. In fact, he was probably the first person to show me unconditional love.

He was also a model of faithfulness. I can't remember a time that he ever showed up to his Sunday School class unprepared. Not that he was the most scintillating teacher in the world. In fact, he had almost no training for that. Vocationally, he worked in the tool and die trade.

But he was for real, and he was also creative. Overall, Walt incarnated Christ for me. And not only for me, but for thirteen other boys in my neighborhood, nine of whom also came from broken homes. Remarkably, eleven of us went on to pursue careers as vocational Christian workers—which is ironic, given that Walt himself completed school only through the sixth grade. It just goes to show that a man doesn't need a Ph.D. for God to use him to shape another man.

Umpiring for Jesus

"Who are you
to judge
another man's
servant?"

Romans 14:4

"You're out! You're Safe!" Our world is full of grand stand umpires, arm-chair quarterbacks, and back seat drivers. For many second-guessing has become second nature.

Instant replays on television sports programs have made expert referees out of all of us. The challenge is "You make the call!"

The message of the Holy Spirit is clearly this: "Don't judge one another, encourage one another, pray for one another, build up one another." That's precisely what I've determined to do.

God doesn't need me to be an umpire. He just wants me to be an encouraging coach.

Lord, help me...
keep me busy rowing with oars You have given me
so I don't have time left for rocking the boat.

Base Camp Basics

As part of her "job" with the Duke University Blue Devils, Mickie Krzyzewski, wife of Duke basketball coach Mike Krzyzewski, interviewed prospective recruits, watched game films with coaches, nursed sick players in her guest room, produced highlight videos for graduating seniors, and ran a summer basketball camp.

While it is her husband's job to coach, she also scolds, praises, and advises young athletes about everything from school to girlfriends. In return, the players affectionately call her "Momma K" or "Mrs. Coach."

Many years ago, however, she wasn't sure that she was suited to the role. Then she ran into Susan Borman, wife of former astronaut Frank Borman. "Some people in this world have to climb a mountain," Susan told her. "To make that climb successful, one person has to go up the mountain, and the other person has to be there at the base camp."

"But why do I have to be the one to stay at the bottom while he gets to climb to the top?" Mickie asked.

Susan just smiled at her knowingly. "Because," she said, "being at the base camp is so much harder."

But to each one of us grace has been given as Christ apportioned it.

Ephesians 4:7

Lord, help me...
make managing the base camp
a mountaintop experience!

Feed My Sheep

Mike Jenkins was flying home from a business conference several years ago when a gentleman was boarded in his wheelchair. Several men lifted him into his seat across the aisle from Mike, buckled him in, and left. He was quadriplegic—paralyzed from the neck down.

After reaching altitude, the flight attendants served beverages, followed by a meal. One of the attendants lowered the tray table in front of the paralyzed man and set his food before him. Mike noticed as the woman seated next to the paralyzed man ate her meal, folded her napkin, and laid her head back to sleep. Right next to her, the gentleman with quadriplegia looked longingly at his food, obviously hungry but unable to feed himself.

Mike leaned over and asked the woman if she was going to help the man. "He's not my responsibility. I don't even know him," she replied.

Mike, extremely upset, called the flight attendant. "Ma'am," he asked, "are you going to help this man eat his meal?"

"Sir," she replied, "it is not the policy of this airline to feed the passengers."

That did it! Mike asked if he might help the man. He responded, "Oh, thank you, I would be so grateful for your help."

Mike stood and asked to exchange places with the woman seated next to the quadriplegic man. She moved grudgingly.

Mike took the napkin, placed it in the gentleman's lap, and salted and peppered his salad.

As Mike cut the meal into bite-size pieces and placed them in the man's mouth, he felt awkward and conspicuous, but also much needed. The man ate with tears running down his cheeks.

The man told Mike of his unfortunate accident, his loneliness, his joys, his struggles, his faith, his hope. His name was Bill.

When my good friend Dave Roever told me that story, I was reminded of all the people who need the good news of the gospel but have no one to feed them. Even today, I hear the words of Jesus to Peter, "Do you love me?… Feed my sheep." (John 21:17)

"My food," said Jesus, *"is to do the will of him who sent me…"*

John 4:34

Lord, help me…
serve others as I would be served.

Someone Is Watching!

On November 8, 1970, Tom Dempsey kicked a 63-yard field goal on the final play of the game to lift his New Orleans Saints to victory.

What makes it more incredible is that Mr. Dempsey had no fingers or toes. He had worked hard to overcome that handicap.

A seven-year-old boy in Kansas saw that kick on TV. It gave him hope. He had just had an accident that resulted in his losing half of his right foot. He determined then not to allow his handicap to stifle his athletic interests.

The young boy's name was Jeff. The last time I talked with Jeff, he was a senior at the University of Kansas where he kicked three field goals over 50 yards.

When Tom Dempsey kicked that field goal, he had no idea that a boy, hurting and discouraged about his future, was watching him. That kick was the inspiration Jeff needed.

Lord, help me...
when the camera is on me,
keep me in focus.

Good Advice

She's twelve years old, and can she ever spell! Jody-Anne Maxwell, from Kingston, Jamaica, correctly spelled "chiaroscurist" (an artist who works in lights and darks) to win the Scripps Howard National Spelling Bee. She won as a seventh grader, but she had spent years preparing.

Besides being intelligent and studious, Jody-Anne, who plans to become a corporate lawyer, is also generous. She shared her prizes, which included $10,000 cash, with the other two contestants from Jamaica, and with her coach and pastor, Glen O. J. Archer.

Shortly after her victory, she was interviewed and asked, "What would you say to other children who want to excel in spelling?"

Her response was both succinct and inspiring: "Trust God, work hard, and never lose sight of your goal."

That is power advice!

"My Father will honor the one who serves me."

John 12:26b

Lord, help me...
remember it's always too soon to quit!

A Season of Renewal

July
a time to search

August
a time to laugh

September
a time to heal

If there is righteousness in the heart, there will be beauty in the character.
If there is beauty in the character, there will be harmony in the house.
If there is harmony in the house, there will be order in the nation.
If there is order in the nation, there will be peace in the world.

Chinese Proverb

July
a time to search

I love you, America. I am ever-grateful that my grandfather, Giovanni Palmieri, immigrated to these United States from Italy as a 16-year-old! He was one of the "tired, the poor" that the Statue of Liberty in New York's harbor welcomed in the early 1900's. He searched for a land of opportunity and found it here.

I'd rather live here than anywhere. I've traveled to Wales, England, France, Switzerland, Germany, and Holland. I love America. I've been to Kenya, South Africa, Botswana, Korea, Brazil, Chile, and Jamaica. But I love America.

We have our problems: the pornography plague, social injustices, political scandals, and spiritual lukewarmness. But the search ends here; America was a land of opportunity for my grandfather just as it is for me and my family today.

I love to loudly and lustily sing about America. I love the flag. I appreciate businesses that fly the "red, white, and blue." I love reciting the Pledge of Allegiance. I get shivers up and down my spine when I say, "one nation, under God, indivisible, with liberty and justice for all."

Lord, help me...
be a flag-waver, not a flag-burner!

One Step at a Time

On a dark, moonless night, a farmer asked his son to go to the barn and get a tool he had left there.

Being very honest, the boy said, "I'm scared. I'm afraid to go because it's so dark out there."

His father handed him a lantern and lit it. The boy held the lantern out in front of him as far as his arm would reach, but it cast its light only a few feet.

"I still can't go," the boy pleaded. "I can't see more than a few feet. I can't see the barn way out there."

His father gave him a word of wisdom, a word of advice, and a word of instruction. "Just walk to the edge of the light."

The son held the lantern in front of him, the light cast its glow a few feet out, and he walked to the edge of the light. When he got to the edge of the light, he discovered that its edge now was out a little farther and he continued to walk toward it. He walked to the edge of the light past the pond, around the stump, and over the fence until he got to the barn. He retrieved the tool.

He turned around and started back toward the house. He walked to the edge of the light, and he walked to the edge of the light again, over the fence, around the stump, and past the pond. Through all the hazards he thought were there, he simply walked to the edge of the light. The son returned safely home to his father.

That's faith. It's walking to the edge of the light. It's going as far as you can see now, then somehow believing and knowing that God will give you the light you need for your next step.

We prefer to walk in the sunshine so we can see the barn and all the obstacles clearly. We'd rather trust in our own might and walk independently. We want to know everything. We want everything to be clear in front of us. But that's just not how this Christian walk is! It's a walk of faith from beginning to end.

We simply walk each day to the edge of the light. And when we get to the edge of the light, we'll discover the same amazing truth the little boy discovered. As we walk to the edge of the light, we'll discover the edge of the light is still a little farther out there. It's safe to take another step. As we walk to the edge of the light, it will indeed continue to provide more light for our path until someday we arrive at the Father's house, safe and secure in heaven.

Even when God seems a million miles away, He's right beside us providing light for our path and hope for our heart. As Jesus said, "...I am the light of the world." (John 9:5) When God seems a million miles away, let's walk by faith and walk to the edge of the light—one step at a time!

Jesus said ... "I am the light of the world."
John 9:5

When All Is Lost

In 1873, Horatio Stafford, a Chicago lawyer, put his wife and four children on a ship headed to France. He intended to follow several weeks later after his business dealings were completed.

On the calm night of November 21, 1873, another ship hit the luxury liner carrying his family. Within 30 minutes, the ship with his wife and four children had gone down. When they realized the ship was sinking, Mrs. Stafford took her four children in her arms. The winds beat and the waves rolled and three of her children slipped off the boat into the icy sea. She was holding her youngest daughter when something pulled the baby away and she was left holding in her hand the baby's gown.

Shortly afterwards, she became unconscious. Sailors from another boat rescued her. After regaining consciousness, Mrs. Stafford was told that all four of her children were gone.

Mr. Stafford had heard about the accident and anxiously awaited news of his family. Ten days passed before he received this two-word cable from his wife: "Saved. Alone."

All that night, Mr. Stafford paced the floors in his home. As he experienced crushing agony and heart-wrenching loss, Mr. Stafford cried out to God, and an incredible peace filled his heart.

Later that morning, he said to his friend who had spent the night with him, "I thank God I am able to trust Him when it costs me something."

A short time later, when he and his wife had been reunited, as Mr. Stafford reflected on those painful, heart-breaking events, he penned the words of this hymn:

When peace, like a river, attendeth my way,
When sorrows like sea billows roll—
Whatever my lot, Thou hast taught me to say,
"It is well, it is well with my soul."

As we walk with God, we're learning to trust Him at all times—especially when it costs us something.

God is our refuge and strength, an ever-present help in trouble.

Psalm 46:1

Lord, help me...
remember that because it costs You everything,
I trust You when it costs me something.

Go 4 It!

He's a video sales associate and he loves going to work every day. His supervisor says of him, "He has a lot of energy and loves to talk to customers. He is one of the most enthusiastic people I work with."

Those with whom he works say that his positive attitude and competitive drive make him one of his company's most consistent sales performers.

I met him in the mid 1990's. It was one of those divine appointments. As I rushed out of a meeting to get back to the office for another appointment, I noticed a blue Pontiac Sunbird parked by the curb with a license plate which read "GO 4 IT."

The driver was getting out as I walked by, so I said, "I really like your license plate." That day I made a new friend, Michael Shevokas.

He told me his story. About fifteen years earlier, while a senior in high school, he slipped on a wet tile floor at an Interstate 80 rest stop. The fall knocked him unconscious and caused severe head trauma, paralysis, and speech loss. He also developed pneumonia and lost more than 70 pounds. Doctors at University of Iowa Hospitals in Iowa City told him he would never walk or talk again.

When I asked him about his recovery, Mike told me, "I have a deep faith in God. God was my guide and my family was my strength."

Mike attacked an intense program of physical and speech therapy. And just five months after the accident, he walked across his high school stage to pick up his diploma. He went on to college and earned a Bachelor's degree in Speech Communication.

His license plate message, GO 4 IT, is his way of encouraging others to never give up, to never stop trying. To never give up though you're hit hard with financial setbacks. To never give up though your body is wracked with pain and growing weaker. To never give up though you've just lost your job. To never give up on your spouse or your marriage. And never, ever give up on yourself or God!

GO 4 IT! Do whatever God is leading you to do, because with God, all things are possible! GO 4 IT!

You'll never finish the race if you don't take that all-important first step.

GO 4 IT! That's Michael Shevokas' message.

*[Jesus said,]
"Everything is
possible for
him who
believes."*

Mark 9:23

Lord, help me...
remember that I have to start the race
before You can finish it.

Two Frogs

Persistence pays. When we are working around the house and getting a little tired, I remind Amy, Jonathan, and Bethany of Robert Schuller's words: "Inch by inch, it's a cinch." Then I repeat the following poem which always manages to lighten our mood. I love this poem because it reminds me that persistence does pay!

Two frogs fell into a can of cream,
or so I've heard told.
The sides of the can were shiny and steep;
the cream was deep and cold.

"Oh, what's the use?" croaked Number I.
"Tis fate; no help's around!
"Good-bye, my friends! Good-bye sad world!"
And weeping still, he drowned.

But Number 2, of sterner stuff,
dog-paddled in surprise.
The while he wiped his creamy face
and dried his creamy eyes.

"I'll swim awhile, at least," he said
(or so I've heard he said);
"It really wouldn't help the world
if one more frog were dead."

An hour or two he kicked and swam,
not once he stopped to mutter.
But kicked and kicked and swam and kicked.
Then hopped out, via butter.

Author unknown

Paying to Volunteer

The 1999 U. S. Senior Open is history. It was an awesome July event as 156 of the world's best senior golfers brought their drivers, irons, and putters to the Des Moines Golf and Country Club. Unquestionably, the fans' favorite golfer was Arnold Palmer. His army was huge!

I'll never forget the front-page headline of the "Des Moines Register": "Palmer's Arrival Thrills Crowd." (The next Sunday I jokingly commented, "As far as I know, I'm the only Senior Open Volunteer who made the front page headlines.") And the crowd was huge! More than 50,000 swarmed the gorgeous green acres for each of the final two rounds.

Amazingly enough, over 3,400 people paid $105 each for the privilege of volunteering at least sixteen hours during the six-day event. The volunteer waiting list was more than 1,000! These volunteers did everything, including parking cars, picking up trash, doing night-time security, chauffeuring the golfers, serving in hospitality centers, scorekeeping, selling food and programs, and being a marshal, as I was. Think of it—paying to volunteer! Why would we do it? Because we believed in the cause, we caught the vision and shared in the excitement of having the premier Seniors' golf event of the year in our city.

Don't wait until the U. S. Senior Open comes to your town. If you're searching for something to do, there's no charge for serving Jesus. It is exciting and rewarding with benefits that are out of this world.

Honor one another above yourselves.

Romans 12:10b

August
a time to laugh

Laughter stimulates creativity, opens the gold mine of imagination, helps us adjust to change, leads to insight, adjusts perspective, bridges differences, reinforces positive thinking, smooths rough edges, teases the mind, and delights the heart. It's a gift that enriches others as well as ourselves. It binds us together.

A genuine smile—the visual component of "making a joyful noise"—communicates in any language.

Most wondrous of all, who has better reason to enjoy laughter in all seasons of life than those of us who "delight in the Lord!"

Lord, help me...
learn to laugh even when it hurts!

When Tin Cans Taste Good

I had to laugh as I read the following in "Pulpit Helps" recently. These are the "Musings of a Country Preacher."

"Attendance at worship last Sunday was a mite poorly. I don't reckon I ought to grumble, because I had a bunch of sick members; and when you add to that all of my shut-ins, we don't have a whole lot more. So, I went ahead and prayed for the sick and shut-ins and preached to the few I had. The only problem was that the echo in the near-empty church building hurt my ears.

"My wife said I needed to get out, take a Sunday afternoon ride, and let the fresh country air clear my head. It made me feel real good inside. What I saw made me rejoice; I saw miracle after miracle!

"Old Hezekiah, who had been deathly sick that morning, was roused up and riding down the highway with his fishing poles. Nothing but a miracle could have rescued him from the jaws of death in such a short time.

"Then there was Rufe's brother. Rufe told me earlier in the day that his brother's back was in such foul shape they were afraid that an operation was going to be necessary. We prayed for him, and lo and behold, at two o'clock there he was at the driving range hitting golf balls. If that wasn't a quick recovery, then I don't know what is.

"All told, about 20 of my sick folks had roused up and were taking nourishment in some form or another. But what made me really happy was to see so many of my shut-ins riding around and enjoying the world.

"Hezekiah's pa, who doesn't attend worship 'cause he can't stand crowds, was headed for the baseball game. Sister Nell's mama, who can't come on account of her kidneys, stood in line for two hours to get into the picture show. Yes, sir, it sure thrilled my heart to see what I saw!

"I ought to have a packed church next Sunday with my sick folks being healed and my shut-ins set free. I just hope they don't overdo themselves and have a relapse before next Sunday. I gotta go now and play with my smallest young'un. He's gonna be a farmer, and I'm gonna be the goat. Tin cans will be easy to eat after what I have swallowed."

Lord, help me...
when people disappoint me, let me be reminded of the
country preacher and graciously swallow hard!

Staying Cool

Have you ever noticed how we do strange things when we're nervous or distracted? According to a Beverly Hills news story, a lady was standing in line to buy an ice cream cone at the Thrifty Drug Store when, to her utter shock and amazement, she realized Paul Newman was right behind her. Even though she was very nervous and excited, she decided to maintain her composure. She purchased the ice cream cone, turned confidently, and exited the store.

When she got outside, she realized she had left the counter without the ice cream cone. She waited a few minutes until she thought the way was clear, then went back into the store to retrieve her ice cream. She approached the counter and discovered the cone was not in the circular receptacle. She stood for a moment, trying to figure out first what had happened to her cone, and second what she ought to do.

She felt a polite tap on her shoulder and turned around to find herself face-to-face with Paul Newman. He asked if she was looking for her ice cream cone.

"Yes," she replied.

Paul Newman calmly explained to her, "You put it in your pocketbook."

He Gave a Warm Blanket

"What did the preacher preach about this morning?" the mother asked of her young son.

"The preacher said that the Lord was going to give us a warm blanket."

"I have never heard anyone preach on that. Are you sure that is what the preacher preached about?"

"Yes, Mommy, I'm sure."

All day long, the mother could not get the thought out of her mind that God was going to give us a "warm blanket."

Finally the mother called a neighbor and asked, "What did the preacher preach about in the morning service?"

The neighbor replied, "He was preaching about the Holy Spirit; he preached about God giving us another Comforter."

Honestly, I don't know what I'd do without the ever-present Comforter. The boy was right, the Holy Spirit is a "warm blanket" and a whole lot more!

In the shelter of your presence you...keep them safe.

Psalm 31:20

Lord, help me...
seek Your presence, where I find real comfort!

God Did It With a Crayon

Be exalted, O God, above the heavens and let your glory be over all the earth.

Psalm 108:5

A parent shared the following wise observation made by her three-year-old daughter:

While riding in the car, my three-year-old daughter Myranda saw a rainbow for the very first time. She was extremely excited as the car topped the hill, giving us a panoramic view of the entire rainbow glistening against the cloudy sky. Her older sister asked her, "Who do you think made that rainbow?"

Without hesitation, Myranda answered, "God!"

Noticing a look of deep thought on her face, I awaited her next response. Unfortunately, it came in the form of one of those dreaded questions three-year-olds are so fond of asking their parents:

"How did God do that?"

Resisting the temptation to explain the molecular structure of a rainbow, I simply answered, "We don't know for sure how God made it."

With that absolute faith only a child can possess, Myranda replied, "Pwobwe wis a quayon!"

God is awesome!

Lord, help me...
remember to thank You for
sometimes coloring outside the lines!

What's That Noise?

The uninitiated new landowner smiled as he exited the hardware store with his new power chain saw guaranteed to cut down several trees per hour. This would make quick work of the trees he wanted to clear from his lot. However, two days later he returned to the store and plopped that chain saw on the counter in a fit of frustration and anger. "This isn't worth a plug nickel," he told the salesman. "You guaranteed it would cut down several trees an hour, and I barely got down one in a whole day."

Somewhat puzzled, the salesman examined the saw. It looked perfectly fine except that the teeth were rather dull and had been damaged some.

The customer followed him outside. The salesman flipped the switch and pulled the cord. The steel-tooth chain whirled around the 24-inch guidebar.

Startled by the deafening noise, the customer jumped back and exclaimed, "What's that noise?"

"'Not by might nor by power, but by my Spirit,' says the Lord Almighty."

Zechariah 4:6

Lord, help me...
know You're the only power source I need!

Finally Forty

"Don't feel bad if you don't put out the candles on your cake with the first blow…professional firefighters can spend hours on a blaze that size." That was just one of many uplifting cards I received during my fortieth birthday party.

When I came into my office, I was greeted with loud cries of mourning and sobbing. I could hardly believe my ears and eyes as I was seated in a wheelchair with an oxygen tank close by. Several dozen roses which had been painted black adorned my office. My wooden figurine of Moses looked different, too. His rod had turned into a black rose. Black "over the hill" balloons, streamers, and bows were everywhere. The staff sang the sad song, "When I've gone the last mile of the way." This message scrolled across my computer screen: "Pastor Palmer, please call Westover Funeral Home to make your arrangements."

As I write this article, I am wearing a black armband with my picture and the words, "In memory of the Rev. J. M. Palmer." The entire team of office personnel, custodians, and pastors wore identical bands during the party.

About those cards—one had a picture of an ancient scroll that had been found in a clay jar in a cave. Inside it read, "Great news! They found your birth certificate."

An optimistic message proclaimed, "40 isn't old! Just ask anyone who's already reached that age! But be sure to speak up and talk in their good ear."

Our creative children's pastor (who was already way past 40) created a homemade card trimmed in black which read, "It is with our deepest regrets that we announce the demise of the youth of the Reverend John M. Palmer. For the past 39 years, Pastor Palmer has enjoyed the excesses of youth. Regrettably, all of this comes to an end on his birthday. Never again will Johnny Come Marching Home Again (limping, dragging, trudging — maybe, but never to march again). Alas, alas, the fair-haired youth of our friend is gone."

But don't you be fooled by all this. Life isn't over; it is just getting started! My black button says, "I'm not over the hill, I'm on a roll." As one card rightly put it, "Don't think of 40 as middle age…think of it as Youth, Part II." I'm finally 40 and feeling sporty.

We had immense fun celebrating this birthday. The best part of turning 40 is looking back at how God has worked His plan for my life these first 40 years and looking ahead with trust and wondering what He has planned for me in the next 40!

Lord, help me...
appreciate the gift of
getting older—and closer to You.

September
a time to heal

The day after our denomination's General Council concluded in Portland, Oregon, our family (all 22 of us), rented three vehicles to visit the magnificent Multnomah Falls and awe-inspiring Mt. Hood ("Mountain Hood," according to Jonathan). Jonathan, his 10-year-old cousin, Betsy Leach, and I decided to climb "Mountain Hood."

We were climbing for quite a while when I noticed Jonathan had no socks. Not surprisingly, he got a blister on his heel. Throughout the vacation, the blister was obviously bothering him. To compensate, he began wearing that particular canvas "slip-on" by putting his toes into the shoe, and bending the heel part of the shoe down, so the back of his foot wouldn't rub against the canvas. It was a sight watching Jonathan run and climb stairs. The "slip-on" slipped off regularly, so he'd go back and pick up his shoe.

He never complained. In fact, he even said, "I'm really glad I have a blister."

"Why, Jonathan, are you glad you have a blister?" we asked. "Because now I know which shoe goes on which foot."

That's what you call turning a negative into a positive!

Lord, help me...
turn my blisters into blessings!

Linda Delbridge was given this grim prognosis: "You're not responding to the laser treatments. We may not be able to save your vision...If your kidney disease progresses as we expect, you will live only another seven years."

She relates, "My daughters were only two and five when specialists at a university medical center delivered their verdicts. My diabetes was threatening the quality of life for my little girls, and my very existence. Terror, fear, anger, helplessness, and horror swept over me.

"For days and years, when I tucked the girls in at night, I wondered if I would see those precious little faces in the morning. I begged God to let me live long enough to see them grow up.

"The struggle to endure was a powerful teacher. I learned that God was at work through friends whose loving supportiveness sustained our family; through a wise superintendent who offered me friendship and a teaching position that impacted my life forever; through our caring doctor and his wife who sent me to a specialist who provided an insulin pump; and through the ophthalmologist whose expertise sustained my vision and whose encouragement sustained my confidence and my spirit.

"I learned that the faces of those we love can't be memorized in detail that satisfies the heart. I learned that God doesn't give us what we ask for, but what we need. It was when I relinquished the struggle to God, knowing His love would surround our family regardless of my health, that I began to mend physically.

"I learned there are many types of healing. I learned that as my physical sight improved, my spiritual vision became more clear. I learned that although it's not always according to our timetable, we do get better; we do heal! My vision and kidney function stabilized. I remained active in the profession to which God called me. I completed two graduate degrees. I rejoiced in being wife and mother and daughter and sister. I prayed. I raised my daughters. I praised the Lord.

"Our younger daughter's summer wedding was a time of celebrating not only God's providence in her life but also His faithful healing presence in my life. God answered my 20-year prayer with 'blessings all mine, with ten thousand beside!'

"I learned that no matter how much I might think God needs my suggestions, He will work His will in His own perfect time and in His own perfect way. It isn't mine to understand; it is mine to trust and abide in Him. Even through loss and grief and confusion and doubt and pain, God is faithful; His everlasting arms uphold me.

"I learned about the Great Physician.

"His is always a time to heal."

Lord, help me...
rest in the knowledge that even when I
can't see You, You see me.

Keep the Faith, Baby

*Let us fix our
eyes on
Jesus, the
author and
perfector of
our faith...*

Hebrews 12:2a

This story from the prisoner-of-war camps in Vietnam has powerfully impacted my life.

As a POW in Vietnam, Colonel Laird Gunnard was beaten and tortured mercilessly. Between interrogations he was forced to kneel in his cramped cell for hours at a time. One day, his Viet Cong captors took him to an interrogation room that he had not seen before. The beating was severe. He crumpled to the floor in a broken, bloody heap.

After the beating, lying with his face to the ground, discouraged and beaten and bleeding, Gunnard wondered if there was any hope, any use of holding out. He opened his eyes and realized he was not the only one who had been there. Someone who had been there before had scrawled four words on the dirt floor: "Keep the faith, baby."

As he looked at those words, "Keep the faith, baby," it gave him encouragement and hope. Someone had been there before. Someone else had gotten out, and he could, too. It was just enough to bolster his faith and bring him through.

Lord, help me...
fix my eyes upon You,
and the things of this world grow faintly dim.

From the "Money" Section

You never know where you'll find a gem. I discovered one in the "Money" section of "USA Today." The newspaper article began, "The one million shareholders of Fidelity's Magellan Fund—the nation's largest stock mutual fund—will be getting a new manager." Morris Smith, after just two years as manager of the $20 billion mutual fund, resigned.

Did this 34-year-old "star" resign because his work wasn't going well? Not at all! One analyst wrote, "Smith ran circles around the ten biggest funds last year."

He gave up hundreds of thousands of dollars of annual income because "Devora and I have always wanted our children to know Israel," says Smith, an Orthodox Jew. He and his family plan to spend at least a year there.

"I want to devote more time to life than to money management," explained Smith. "Life" for him is his religion and his family. Morris Smith could walk away from the lucrative pay, power, and prestige of the corporate world because he had his priorities properly ranked. The picture caption read "Bound for Israel."

Would you be willing to walk away from prosperity, power, and a promotion if you felt these things were hindering you from devoting yourself to the pursuit of God?

Lord, help me...
remember I'm not here for a good
time, but a for a good eternity.

"For where your treasure is, there your heart will be also."

Matthew 6:21

First Things First

Feeling alone and wanting companionship, a woman went to a pet store and purchased a parrot. With excitement, she took her new pet home and waited for it to talk. After a day, the parrot had not said a word, so she went back to the store and reported, "My new parrot hasn't said one word yet."

"Does it have a mirror?" asked the pet store owner. "Parrots like to be able to look at themselves in a mirror."

So she bought a nice mirror, returned home, and placed it in the parrot's cage.

Later that day, the lady returned to the pet store and announced that the bird still wasn't talking. "What about a ladder?" the storekeeper suggested. "Parrots enjoy walking up and down a ladder."

So she purchased the best ladder in the store and returned home.

When the pet store owner arrived for work the next morning, the lady stood waiting for him. Noticeably upset, she complained vigorously that the parrot still was not talking. The owner told her that parrots talk more when they're relaxed. He explained, "Birds enjoy relaxing on a swing. Why not buy a swing for your parrot?"

She bought the swing and went home.

Later that afternoon, she called the store to announce the bird had died. "I'm terribly sorry to hear that," consoled the owner. "Did the bird ever say anything before it died?"

"Yes," replied the lady. "The parrot asked, 'Don't they sell any food down there?'"

Like the parrot, we have "mirrors" with which we seek to take care of our physical bodies. We have "ladders" by which we seek to climb to higher social, educational, and economic heights. We have "swings" for pleasure and relaxation.

But are we putting first things first by feeding our spirits through the reading of God's Word, worship, and prayer?

Lord, help me...
with a gentle nudge when I fail to put first
things first, like starting the day with You!

Never Give Up

Forgetting what is behind and straining toward what is ahead . . . I press on toward the goal . . .

Philippians 3:13

Winston Churchill wasn't a very good student at Harrow School. In fact, some historians say that if his father had not been the famed Lord Randolph Churchill, he probably would have been expelled.

However, he did complete his work at Harrow, went on to a university, and then embarked on a brilliant and illustrious career in the British military, serving in both Africa and India.

At the age of 67, he was elected Prime Minister of the British Empire. With great courage, he in turn brought courage to his nation through his speeches and leadership during the dark days of WWII.

Toward the very end of his term as Prime Minister, he was invited back to address the young boys at Harrow.

In announcing the coming of their great alumnus, the headmaster said, "Young gentlemen, the greatest orator of our time, perhaps of all time, our Prime Minister will be here in a few days to address you. It will behoove you to listen carefully to whatever sound advice he may bring to you at that time."

The great day arrived, the building was spotlessly clean, and the boys were looking their finest. Following a glowing and rather lengthy introduction, Sir Winston Churchill stood up, all five feet five inches, 235 pounds of him, acknowledged the effusive introduction, and then delivered this brief but moving speech:

"Young men, never give up.

"Never give up.

"Never give up.

"Never,

"Never,

"Never,

"Never."

And he sat down.

Lord, help me...
grant me power to persist,
courage to continue, and faith to follow.

Par for the Course

Three senior golfers complained continually. "The fairways are too long," said one.

"The hills are too high," said another.

"The bunkers are too deep," complained the third.

Finally an 80-year-old put things into perspective. "At least," he noted sagely, "we're on the right side of the grass."

Lord, help me...
make the best of it,
even when I get the worst of it.

You Can Make It

When we celebrate Amy's birthday, we also celebrate Debbie's—they share the same birthday. I'll never forget the day Amy was born—September 3, 1980. Early that morning Debbie awakened me with these words, "It's time." Upon arriving at O'Bleness Memorial Hospital, Debbie was quickly admitted and taken immediately to the delivery cubicle. While I had faithfully attended the Lamaze child-birthing classes, I was totally unprepared for the real thing. As Debbie's labor pains increased, I tried hard to support and encourage her, wiping her brow with a cool cloth, holding her hand, and telling her how much I loved her and how proud I was of her.

By six o'clock that morning Debbie was tired of the labor and said despairingly, "I can't make it. I can't go any further. I can't deliver this baby."

My inane response? "Well, honey, you can't stop now. You can't live the rest of your life nine months pregnant. You have to keep going."

"I can't do it," she remonstrated. "I can't make it."

Just then, I spotted a television and turned it on. You'll never guess what we saw and heard. A well-known singer was singing Mike Murdock's encouraging song, "You can Make It." With a huge smile she sang, "This trial you're going through, God's gonna show you just what to do...You're not in this thing alone...You can make it."

When Debbie felt she simply couldn't go on, God gave her the strength to do it. Debbie kept calm and Amy was born, much to our delight and joy.

A Season of Celebration

October
a time to gather

November
a time to harvest

December
a time for peace

If we believe in a progressive, forward-moving existence with
wonderful potential, we will be living an interesting life.
A big difference between happiness and misery, effectiveness and
uselessness cannot be blamed on circumstances or other people.
The condition of your mind creates your reality.

Sir John Templeton

October

a time to gather

Driving home from church on a Wednesday evening, we turned on the radio to hear the 10:00 news. What we heard just before the newscast was the weekly Powerball drawing. Jonathan, in his inimitable eight-year-old way, asked, "How come people play the lottery?"

I gave the first answer that popped into my mind, "Because some people want to get rich quick."

His insightful response surprised us: "They need to get saved, then they'll get riches in Heaven."

Our culture puts a lot of pressure on us to earn more money and accumulate more things. When John D. Rockefeller was asked, "How much money does it take to satisfy a man?" he replied, "Just a little bit more."

We all know that "we can't take it with us." But if we're not careful, it takes us with it. The value of one's net worth is not as important as how one values his net worth.

In taking to heart Jonathan's words of wisdom concerning riches in Heaven, I've resolved to make sure that I'm continuing to add to my portfolio there!

Lord, help me...
make my Heavenly 401K outperform my earthly one.

Better Not to Know

Dr. Robert Schuller, Senior Pastor of the Crystal Cathedral, tells a story about sitting on a plane next to a fellow with his nose in a book. Finally, the man looked over at Dr. Schuller and recognized him from a picture on one of the books he had with him. The fellow asked him what he did for a living and Dr. Schuller replied that he wrote books. The man quickly responded that he wrote books too—on mathematics.

Dr. Schuller explained he wrote books on "Possibility Thinking" but admitted that they probably had nothing in common as "in mathematics it doesn't matter whether you are a possibility thinker or an impossibility thinker. Two plus two equals four regardless of whether you are a negative or a positive person."

"Well, I'm not so sure about that," his seat partner interrupted. "Let me tell you about myself. My name is George Danzig, and I am in the Physics Department at Stanford University. I've just returned from Vienna as the American delegate to the International Mathematics Convention, appointed by the President. I was a senior at Stanford during the Depression; we knew, when the class graduated, we'd all be joining unemployment lines. There was a slim chance that the top man in class might get a teaching job, but that was about it. I wasn't at the head of my class, but I hoped that if I were able to score a perfect paper on the final exam, I might be given a job opportunity."

He paused to swallow, blinking behind his glasses. "I studied so hard for that exam, I ended up making it to class late. When I arrived, the others were already hard at work. I was embarrassed and just picked up my paper and slunk to my desk. I sat down and worked the eight problems on the test paper and then started in on the two that were written on the board. Try as I might, I couldn't solve either one of them. I was devastated; out of ten problems, I had missed two for sure. But just as I was about to hand in the paper, I took a chance and asked the professor if I might have a couple days to work on the two I had missed. I was surprised when he agreed, and I rushed home and plunged into those equations with a vengeance. I spent hours and hours, and finally solved one of them. I never could get the other. And when I turned in that paper, I knew I had lost all chance of a job. That was the blackest day of my life.

"The next morning, I was awakened by a pounding on the door. It was my professor, all dressed up and very excited. 'George, George,' he kept shouting, 'you've made mathematics history!' Well, I didn't know what he was talking about. And then he explained.

"I had come to class late and had missed his opening remarks. He had been encouraging the class to keep trying, not to give up if they found some of the problems difficult. 'Don't put yourself down,' he had said. 'Remember there are classic, unsolvable problems. Even Einstein was unable to unlock their secrets.' And then he had written two of these "unsolvable" problems on the blackboard.

Jesus replied, "What is impossible with man is possible with God."

Luke 18:27

When I came in, I didn't know they were unsolvable. I thought they were part of my exam, and I was determined that I could work them properly. And I solved one! It was published in the "International Journal of Higher Mathematics," and my professor gave me a job as his assistant. I've been at Stanford for 43 years now."

He stopped and looked piercingly at the pastor. "Dr. Schuller, I'm just going to ask you one question. If I had come to class on time, do you think I would have solved that problem? I don't."

Lord, help me...
when there is no solution,
help me seek it lovingly!

Give It All Away

A legend tells of a man who was lost in a desert and on the verge of dying of thirst.

He stumbled on until he came to an abandoned house. Outside the dilapidated, windowless, deserted shack stood a pump. He began to pump furiously, but no water came from the well. Then he noticed a small corked jug with a message written on its side: "You have to prime the pump with water. And please, fill the jug again before you leave." When he pulled the cork, he saw that the jug was full of water.

Should he pour it down the rusty pump? What if it didn't work? Then all the water would be gone. If he drank the water from the jug, at least he could be sure he would not immediately die of thirst.

What a problem! What a decision!

Deciding to follow the advice on the note, the man poured the whole jug of clean water down the rusty old pipes and proceeded to pump furiously. Sure enough, water gushed out. Within a few seconds, he had all he needed to drink.

Satisfied, he filled the jug again, corked it, and added his own words beneath the instructions on the jug. "Believe me, it really works. You have to give it all away before you can get anything back."

. . .but the righteous give without sparing.

Proverbs 21:26b

Leaving Footprints

Running on the beach of North Carolina's Outer Banks is in itself a tiring, exhilarating experience.

When I had run as far as I could and had collapsed into that salty surf, there was not one sign of my morning's run. Those powerful Atlantic waves had washed away my footprints as quickly as I had put them in the sand. Who would ever know that I had gotten up at sunrise, run my legs to a point of exhaustion, and felt "at one with the universe"? Who would ever know?

In our competitive living, so often it seems important that our peers know what we've done! Personal accomplishments lose their value unless they are lauded and recognized in the arena of "success." So few experiences hold worth on their face value.

In the Sermon on the Mount, we are taught to "Be careful not to do your 'acts of righteousness' before men, to be seen by them. If you do, you will have no reward from your Father in heaven." Although "acts of righteousness" refers to giving money or helping the needy, the term might be expanded to include our current-day "acts of ministry."

It has become the American way to be "bigger and better than." We drive new and improved cars with bigger features and better gas mileage; we live in bigger and better houses with bigger and better energy-saving devices; we attend bigger and better churches with bigger and better choirs and sound systems.

In our society's bigger-and-better syndrome, we have forgotten about BEST.

When I have done my best, I may or may not be bigger and better, but I will have excelled and can be counted worthy. When I have done my best, I do not need the applause or the rewards of man, for my father in heaven sees and knows the desires of my heart. When I have done my best, I may be tired and exhausted, but I can hear the clear, sure "Well Done!"

When we can stand before the throne of God and know that we have given all for His Kingdom, it does not matter who on earth knows what we have done.

Yes, when you have done the best you can, there may be no footprints in the sand. But who needs them?

Author unknown

". . .what is due me is in the Lord's hand, and my reward is with my God."

Isaiah 49:4b

Lord, help me...
echo the words of Emily Dickenson:
"If I can help one fainting robin unto its nest again,
I shall not live in vain."

Who Is Applauding?

Many years ago, a young couple had their first child, a boy. As the boy began to grow, they noticed his musical talent. He could play the violin. They searched for the best possible teacher for him. They heard about an old Swiss maestro who used to teach but who had now retired. They decided to try anyway, and took their boy to see him.

When the maestro heard the boy play, he recognized the ability and decided to teach him. The boy was just eight years old. For ten years, his teacher worked with him almost every day. Then came the time for his debut. His parents booked Carnegie Hall. The press and all the important people came. The lights dimmed and the boy came out on stage. From the very first note until the end, he held the crowd mesmerized. When he finished, the people stood to their feet and filled the hall with cheers and applause. Yet the boy ran off the stage in tears.

The stage manager yelled, "Get back out there! They love you! They're all cheering and clapping."

The boy replied, "There is one who is not."

The manager ran out on stage and came back quickly. He said, "Okay, one old man is not applauding. You can't worry about what one old man thinks when the world loves you."

The boy answered, "But you don't understand. That one man is my teacher."

Sow Seeds, Reap Fruit

A young woman, a great lover of flowers, had set out a rare vine at the base of a stone wall. It grew vigorously, but it did not seem to bloom. Day after day she cultivated it and tried every possible way to coax it to bloom.

One morning as she examined the vine with obvious disappointment, her invalid neighbor called to her and said, "You can't imagine how much I have been enjoying the blooms of that vine you planted." The owner followed her neighbor's gaze and on the other side of the wall saw a mass of blooms. The vine had crept through the crevices and produced flowers on the other side!

How often we think our efforts are thrown away because we do not see fruit. We need to learn that in God's service our prayers, our toil, our crosses are never in vain. They will bear fruit and hearts will receive blessings and joy—sometime, somewhere.

"Each tree is recognized by its own fruit."

Luke 6:44a

Lord, help me...
as branches to the vine,
my soul would cling to You, Lord.

What Vacancy?

. . .my days
have no
meaning.

Job 7:16b

Someone shared with me the following story about a tiny general store in the country which he visited on occasion.

The proprietor of the general store out in the country had a clerk named Jake who I always thought was the laziest man ever created. Then one day, I noticed that Jake was nowhere around.

I asked, "Where's Jake?"

The proprietor answered, "Oh, he retired."

"Retired? Then what are you doing about filling his vacancy?"

The owner replied, "Jake didn't leave no vacancy!"

These words have stayed with me a long time. I think often of how sad it might be if the final judgment of my efforts was "He didn't leave no vacancy."

Lord, help me...
wear out before I rust out.

Water Beetle

Cecil B. DeMille, the famous motion-picture producer, was a man of great talents and keen insights. He liked to get away by himself at times to think through a problem. One such time when faced with several vexing personal problems, he took a canoe out on a lake in Maine.

After a while, the canoe floated towards shore to a place where the water was only a few inches deep. Looking down, DeMille saw that beetle-like bugs crowded the bottom. As he watched, one of the water beetles came to the surface and slowly crawled up the side of the canoe. Finally, reaching the top, the beetle grasped fast to the wood and died.

DeMille soon forgot the beetle and his thoughts went back to his own problems. Several hours later, he happened to notice the beetle again and saw that in the hot sun its shell had become very dry and brittle. As he watched, it slowly split open and a new form emerged—a dragonfly which took to the air, its scintillating colors flashing in the sunlight.

The winged insect flew farther in an instant than the water beetle had crawled in days. Then it circled back and swooped down to the surface of the water. DeMille noticed its shadow on the water. The water beetles below might have seen it too, but now their erstwhile former companion dwelt in a world beyond their comprehension. They still lived in their limited world while their winged cousin had gained for himself all the freedom between earth and sky.

Later, when DeMille related this experience, he concluded with a very penetrating question: "Would the great Creator of the universe do that for a water beetle and not for a human being?"

Sparky Was a Loser

Sparky was a loser. When he was a little boy, the other children called him "Sparky" after a comic-strip horse named Sparkplug. Sparky never did manage to shake that nickname.

School was all but impossible for Sparky. He failed every subject in the eighth grade. Every subject! He flunked physics in high school. Receiving a flat zero in the course, he distinguished himself as the worst physics student in his school's history.

Throughout his youth, Sparky was socially awkward. He was not actually disliked by the other youngsters. No one cared that much. He was astonished if a classmate ever said hello to him outside school hours. There is no way to tell how he might have done at dating. In high school, Sparky never once asked a girl out. He was too afraid of being turned down.

Sparky was a loser. He, his classmates, everyone knew it. So he rolled with it. Sparky made up his mind early in life that if things were meant to work out, they would. Otherwise, he would content himself with what appeared to be inevitable mediocrity.

But this is "the rest of the story."

One thing was important to Sparky: drawing. He was proud of his own artwork. Of course, no one else appreciated it. In his senior year of high school, he submitted some cartoons to the editors of his class yearbook. Almost predictably, Sparky's drawings were rejected.

While the young man had stoically rationalized virtually all of his failures up to this time, he was rather hurt by the general ignorance of what he believed was his one natural talent. In fact, he was so convinced of his artistic ability that he decided right then and there to become a professional artist.

Upon graduating from high school, he wrote a letter to Walt Disney Studios, a letter indicating his qualifications to become a cartoonist for Disney. Shortly, he received an answer, a form letter requesting that he send some samples of his artwork. Subject matter was suggested. For instance, a Disney cartoon character "repairing" a clock by shoveling the springs and gears back inside.

Sparky drew the proposed cartoon scene. He spent a great deal of time on that and the other drawings. A job with Disney would be impressive, and Sparky had many doubters to impress.

He mailed the form and his drawings to Disney Studios. Sparky waited. And one day the reply came.

Deep down, Sparky probably expected to be rejected. He had always been a loser, and this was simply one more loss.

He did not get the job.

So Sparky decided to write his life story in cartoons. He described his childhood self, the little boy loser, the chronic underachiever, in a cartoon character the whole world now knows. He created the "Peanuts" comic strip and the little cartoon boy whose kite would never fly—Charlie Brown.

For the boy who failed the entire eighth grade, the young artist whose work was rejected by Walt Disney Studios and by his own high school yearbook, that young man was "Sparky" Charles Monroe Schultz.

November
a time to harvest

During the Depression, W. L. Stiger, a Methodist pastor in Boston, struggled to put together a Thanksgiving message. Although much around him was bleak, he began to recount his blessings.

He remembered a school teacher with whom he'd had no contact for many years. She had inspired and instilled in him a love for Tennyson's poetry, for which he was very grateful.

Though a very busy pastor, he wrote her a note expressing his thanks and gratitude. A short time later, he received this reply:

"My dear Willie:

"I cannot tell you how much your note meant to me. I am in my 80's, living alone in a small room, cooking my own meals, lonely and, like the last leaf of autumn, just lingering behind. You will be interested to know that I taught in public school for 50 years and yours is the first note of appreciation I have ever received. It came on a blue, cold morning, and it cheered me as nothing has in many years."

Lord, help me...
create many of my own "Kodak" moments.

Finish What You've Started

When Dr. A. J. Cronin was suffering from a great physical malady, he decided to take some months off from his medical practice and go into the Scottish Highlands. While there, he began to think about the novel he had always wanted to write.

For three months, he wrote and wrote and wrote, but the more he wrote, the more discouraged he became. It just wasn't coming together. Finally one rainy Scotland day, in sheer desperation and utter discouragement, he took all the hundreds of pages he had written, went outside, and threw them into a large trash can where the rain quickly soaked them all. Dejected, he walked down to the lake where he met an old farmer with whom he shared what he had just done.

The farmer replied thoughtfully, "Doctor, you are a lot smarter than I am. You're probably right and I am probably wrong, but let me tell you what I think. You see this piece of land that I'm digging? My dad started digging this a few years ago. It doesn't drain very well. It's not very good land, but my dad and I both have a feeling that if we dig on this hard enough and long enough, we're going to get something good out of it."

As the farmer continued working the land that everybody else had discarded, Dr. Cronin turned to walk back to his little house. As raindrops fell on his head, a new determination rose up in his heart. He marched to that trash can, took out all those soaking papers, dried them on the kitchen stove, and began to write again.

Several months later, he sent the manuscript to a publisher and then forgot all about it—until the day he received notice that his book would be published.

"Hatter's Castle" was subsequently published in nineteen different languages and dramatized around the world. We enjoy that powerful literary work because a man returned to a trash can and pulled out the soggy papers, dried them off, and finished what he had started.

"'After this I will return and rebuild...'"

Acts 15:16a

Lord, help me...
fight the good fight,
finish the race, and keep the faith.

An Unlikely Blessing

Many years ago, citizens in Enterprise, Alabama, erected an unusual monument honoring the Mexican boll weevil. Here's why.

In 1895, the boll weevil began to destroy the major crop of Coffee County: cotton.

In their desperation to survive, farmers had to diversify, and by 1919 the county's peanut crop was many times what cotton had been at its height. In that year of prosperity, a fountain and monument were built.

The accompanying inscription reads: "In profound appreciation of the boll weevil and what it has done as the herald of prosperity, this monument was erected by the citizens of Enterprise, Coffee County, Alabama."

Out of a time of struggle and crisis had come new growth and success. Out of adversity had come blessing.

When your "cotton" is ruined, look for the "peanuts."

Lord, help me...
see the boll weevil as a blessing in disguise,
and then You can just keep on "bugging" me with blessings!

A Grateful Heart

Matthew Henry, the famous Bible scholar, was once accosted by thieves and robbed of his money. He wrote these words in his diary:

"Let me be thankful first because I was never robbed before; second, although they took my purse (money), they did not take my life; third, because although they took my all, it was not much; and fourth, because it was I who was robbed, not I who robbed."

A thankful heart doubles our blessings, causing us to enjoy them twice—when we receive them and when we remember them.

. . just as you received Christ Jesus as Lord, continue to live in him . . . overflowing with thankfulness.

Colossians 2:6-7

Lord, help me...
be twice the blessing to others.

Unseen Harvest

One of my all-time best teachers was such a good teacher because his actions and his words conveyed the same message. I've never met another man who was as consistently godly as he. He taught what was right and he lived what was taught. I knew this teacher well: he was my dad! He taught me to keep going.

When Dad graduated from Central Bible Institute in 1942, he went back to his hometown, New Castle, Pennsylvania, with a burning desire to plant a new church. After obtaining permission from his home church pastor and board, he sought a suitable building. He located a one-room frame building that once had been a school. With his own money, he rented the building, fixed it up, and printed flyers to announce the starting of a new church. Excitedly, he went door to door inviting the neighbors.

Two days before the first service, his pastor called him to his office and informed him that the deacon board had decided that Dad should not start the church. Much to Dad's surprise, they had asked another member of the church to be the pastor. The really hard part was when he asked Dad to give him the key to the building—the building Dad had rented, repaired, and renovated all by himself.

He was very disappointed and could sense some bitterness seeping into his spirit. But he forgave and determined to go on. He remained a faithful and loyal member of his home church, teaching

Sunday School and working with the young people. He and Mom got married about a year later, and the two of them moved fifty miles north to Meadville, where he planted a church and pastored for nine years. That's where I was born.

Thirty-nine years and five churches later, he was attending a pastor's meeting in Ohio. There he met Curtis Powell, who related his testimony to my father. He said, "Thirty-eight years ago, I was unsaved and an alcoholic. A preacher rented a one-room school building and started a church. My children began attending and invited me to the last night of Vacation Bible School. Shortly thereafter, I was saved, delivered from alcohol, and later became a deacon in that church. Sometime later, God called me to pastor."

Tears were streaming down Dad's face as he listened to this incredible story, and no wonder! Mr. Powell was saved, in part, because Dad had planted the seed. Refusing to be bitter, Dad kept doing, and God gave him forty-four years of fruitful and rewarding ministry.

And I'll never forget his admonition as he finished telling me that story: "Remember, John, our disappointments may become God's appointments. So just keep going."

And, by His grace, I have!

...Always give yourselves fully to the work of the Lord, because you know that your labor in the Lord is not in vain.
Corinthians 15:58

Rejoice Always

Dr. Samuel Shoemaker tells the story of an elderly woman who was knocked down by a tire that flew off a passing truck. The accident left her with a broken hip and confined her to a small room for the rest of her days. Some would have grown bitter or at least impatient with such circumstances.

Not this lady! When Dr. Shoemaker stood by her in the hospital, she looked up from her bed of intense pain and said with a wonderful smile, "Well, I wonder what God has for me to do here."

What a beautiful, positive attitude!

When trouble bowls you over, when you are at the bottom emotionally, it's still a matter of choice; no one else can decide for you. You alone must choose whether you will let trouble lick you, or whether you will take courage and, with God's help, lick the trouble.

There is nothing in this world that can happen to you but what, with God's help and with a positive attitude, you can come out on top.

Lord, help me...
even if I'm flat on my back, remind
me not to confuse attitude with altitude—
I can still have one without the other!

Always Give Thanks

Dr. Alexander Whyte of Edinburgh was famous for his pulpit prayers. He always found something for which to thank God, even in bad times. One stormy morning, a gloomy member of his congregation thought to himself, "The preacher will have nothing for which to thank God on a wretched morning like this."

But Whyte began his prayer, "We thank Thee, O God, that it is not always like this."

Dante Gabriel Rossetti summed it up well when he observed, "The worst moment for the atheist is when he is really thankful and has nobody to thank."

...give thanks in all circumstances...
Thessalonians 5:18

Lord, help me...
always look for the best in everything
because I may just find it!

The Unsung Heroes

Tom Friedman writes a weekly article about his experiences as a small businessman. Recently, he praised the "unsung heroes" of his and many other small businesses.

"During the past couple of weeks, I have opened my eyes to some of the true heroes of small businesses: the spouses. Between the moving and the grand opening of our new building, I have logged many hours at work and not nearly enough hours at home…But Joanne (my wife) has been very understanding and supportive, and not just in a passive way.

"In addition to being the primary caregiver for our four children, she has been at every bank-sponsored function…She has taken an active interest in my career, my small business. Joanne typifies to me a large group of unsung heroes, the spouses of small business owners.

"Owning or managing a small business puts a strain on any marriage. There are long hours while tending the business, Saturday and Sunday emergency calls, and financial stresses. One example is our security system. The past two weeks have been spent working through a couple of bugs in the system. The alarm would go off, and someone from the bank had to meet the police at the building to ensure it was just a false alarm. The alarm didn't care if you had just settled in for supper or were walking out the door to church…it had to be answered.

Spouses of small business owners (and employees) understand and keep supper warm or agree to take the four kids to church alone. A heroic act in anyone's book!

"Small businesses do not always have the resources to provide the other financial benefits of a larger company. Often a pension plan is lacking and occasionally basic health insurance coverage. During lean times, business owners are often required to dig deep into their pockets to support the business. I have known a lot of small business owners who have forgone their scheduled paycheck so that the business bills could be paid. A sacrifice that their employees wouldn't understand, but their spouses do.

"Spouses of small business owners have realized that small businesses are like babies. They need lots of attention, lots of hand-holding and sometimes need changing in the middle of the night. They also eat a lot—of cash! So, to Joanne and all the other spouses who realize that the attention span of the ones they love can easily be distracted by the business, thank you. Without your love and support, we couldn't chase our business dreams."

Lord, help me...
appreciate the unsung heroes in my life.

Young Spencer

*"Was no one
found to
return and
give praise to
God. . .?"*

Luke 17:18

For many years, Northwestern University at Evanston, Illinois, had a student volunteer life-saving crew.

On September 8, 1860, the Lady Elgin, a crowded passenger steamer, foundered off the shore of Lake Michigan just above Evanston. As students gathered on shore, one of them spotted in the distance a woman clinging to wreckage far out in the breakers. Edward W. Spencer, a student at Garrett Biblical Institute, threw off his coat, swam through the heavy waves, and succeeded in getting the drowning woman back to shore safely.

Sixteen times during that day young Spencer braved those fierce waves, rescuing seventeen persons. Then he collapsed in a delirium of exhaustion.

Ed Spencer slowly recovered from the exposure and exertion of that day, but never completely. With broken health, he lived quietly, unable to enter upon his chosen lifework of the ministry, but exemplifying the teachings of Jesus Christ in his secluded life. He died in California at the age of eighty-one.

In the newspaper notice of his death, it was noted that not one of those seventeen rescued persons ever came to thank him.

God Uses Our Trials

On display in the French Academy of Science is a shoemaker's awl. It looks ordinary, but behind that little awl lie both tragedy and victory.

One day it fell from the shoemaker's table and struck the eye of his nine-year-old son. Within weeks, the child was blind in both eyes and had to attend a special school for the sightless.

At that time, the blind read by using large carved wooden blocks that were clumsy and awkward to handle. When he grew up, the shoemaker's son devised a new reading system of punched dots on paper. And to do it, Louis Braille used the same awl that had blinded him.

I have learned to be content whatever the circumstances.

Philippians 4:11b

Lord, help me...
even in the darkness,
see beyond my circumstances!

December
a time to peace

A few years ago, some children were putting on the Christmas play. To show the radiance of the new-born Savior, an electric light bulb was hidden inside the manger. All the stage lights were to be turned off so that only the brightness of the manger could be seen, but the boy who controlled the lights got confused—all the lights went out!

It was a tense moment...broken only when one of the young shepherds said in a loud stage whisper..."Hey, you switched off Jesus!"

This month we celebrate Christmas, the birth of Jesus, our Savior and Lord. We're very busy with lots of exciting things to do: shopping, wrapping, baking, decorating, church musicals, company parties, and family and neighborhood get-togethers. And I for one, love it all!

Could it be, though, that the honored guest of the birthday celebration has been left out? Has he been rudely ignored and relegated to a few minutes of worship on Christmas Eve? Do our children hear more about Santa than the Savior? Have we temporarily "switched off" Jesus?

This holiday season, let's keep Christ at the center of Christmas.

Lord, help me...
let the light of Jesus shine through me this Christmas.

Missing the Point

...faith comes from hearing the message, and the message is heard through the word of Christ.

Romans 10:17

One December day after repeated attempts, Orville and Wilbur Wright finally did what no human had ever done before. Off the sand dunes of Kitty Hawk, North Carolina, they flew their airplane. Elated and proud, they wired their sister Katherine, "We have actually flown 120 feet. Will be home for Christmas."

Ecstatic, Katherine ran down the street and placed the telegram, the news scoop of the century, into the hand of the city editor of the local newspaper. He read it and smiled. "Well, well. How nice. The boys will be home for Christmas."

Sorry, Mr. Editor, you missed the point!

Could it be that some of us miss the point of this holiday? We shop, wrap, exchange, party, and bake. Some of us end up dead tired, feeling squeezed and emptied like a used tube of toothpaste.

The point of this season is Jesus! In the next few days, let's re-read the story of His miraculous birth. Let's refresh ourselves in His presence. Let's allow Him to renew us physically, emotionally, and spiritually. Make a point to attend a Christmas Sunday School program and experience the wonder of that night long ago through the eyes of children. Treat yourself to a Christmas choir concert.

Whatever you do, attend a Christmas Eve worship service with friends and family. May your Christmas this season be filled with love, joy, and peace.

Gift of Love

It was Christmas Eve, 1935, the height of the Depression. A young widow and her six-year-old son prepared to celebrate Christmas. There would be no candy and no purchasing gifts this year. Even supper, which usually had been a lavish feast, would be very plain.

And the gifts, they were simple, too. The mother had knit a pair of mittens for her son and herself. They weren't knitted as perfectly as she would have liked, but they would have to do. As she called her little boy for supper, he raced to the bedroom and came back with a gift wrapped in newspaper. His eyes danced and sparkled with excitement and anticipation as he gave it to his mother, saying, "Open it, Mommy, open it!"

The mother carefully removed the newspaper wrapping to find an old cigar box. She opened it slowly, savoring the moment. Inside the box she found a shiny copper penny and a piece of paper on which he had written a message in crayon: "i luv yu mome."

Tears welled in her eyes as she read these words over and over again. All she could say as she hugged him was, "Thank you. Thank you. This is the best gift I've ever received."

And so a mother's and son's bleak Christmas Eve was transformed into a joyous celebration of love, made possible because each gave to the other a "gift of love."

Lord, help me...
tell my loved ones how much
I love them each day of the year.

Truths From the Turnpike

I was wrapping up an intense counseling session on Tuesday, December 13, about 4:10 p.m., when the call came to my office. It was Bill, my brother-in-law, telling me that my mom had been in a one-car accident and had not survived. I couldn't believe what I was hearing. She was on her way home to New Castle, Pennsylvania, from my sister's house when it happened.

On the Ohio Turnpike, between gates 13 and 14, at mile-marker 196.1, Mom left earth for heaven! Thankfully, she didn't suffer. The coroner's report indicated she had a heart attack and died before the car was destroyed by fire. We would have been with Mom on Christmas Day, but God had other plans. She spent Christmas in heaven with Dad!

The days after my mother's terrible turnpike accident were difficult and painful. But the grace of God, the joy of Jesus, the strength of His Spirit, and the encouragement of our church family sustained us.

And we learned vital lessons. The first has to do with things: Every physical thing will someday either decay, rust, or burn. Every human body, every house in the inner city and every house at the country club, all the boats, snowmobiles and cars and trucks, our TVs and CD players and radios—every material thing in this world will be gone someday.

A few days after the funeral, I went to see Mom's car. Nothing was left inside the car—no plastic, no seats, nothing left but raw metal.

Everything that was not metal had been burned completely. This had been the nicest and newest car Mom had ever owned; she had loved that little car!

Just as that car suddenly lost its value, all our stocks and bonds, all our investments, anything material that we possess or own someday will be gone. They will be of zero value—except for investments in the eternal.

So how are you spending your money? How are you spending your time? Is shopping for Christmas gifts more exciting than sharing yourself? If this were to be your last Christmas on earth, would you be assured of spending your next one in heaven?

In the days following Mom's death, I learned a second truth from the turnpike: God will bring us safely through every trial.

When we went to the accident site, we picked up a few items that had flown out of Mom's car, but nearly everything had been consumed by the fire. Later, friends also visited the site. Quite a distance from the car, they found Mom's winter coat which had been badly burned. There was nothing left of it to save. They tried reaching into the pockets but couldn't because the plastic pocket liners had been melted together. Our good friends Mark and Jan Ford, however, tore the pocket apart, reached inside, and found one of Mom's silk hankies.

Do not store up for yourselves treasures on earth, where moth and rust destroy...But lay up for yourselves treasures in heaven...

Matthew 6: 19-20a

Miraculously, it had not been burned and did not smell of fire. Mark and Jan framed it and gave it to us on the day of Mom's funeral. Still today, when I see this hankie, I think of how it was spared from the fire and kept safe, and how in the same way my mother's spirit is safe. Mom's body was burned beyond recognition, but God saved her spirit and delivered her safely to our eternal home.

Mom did make it home on December 13, 1994; she made it to her eternal home. She didn't make it to New Castle, Pennsylvania, but she made it to heaven. She left earth between gates thirteen and fourteen on the turnpike and entered heaven through the pearly gates. She went home to heaven because she was ready to meet the Lord—Jesus Christ was her Savior! The greatest truth from the turnpike is this: you and I will also go to heaven if we are ready to meet the Lord when we die.

Lord, help me...
make sure I'm traveling
on the highway to heaven!

Keeping His Word

It was the day after Christmas at a church in San Francisco. The pastor of the church was looking over the creche when he noticed that the baby Jesus was missing from among the figures. Immediately he turned and went outside and discovered a little boy with a red wagon, and in the wagon was the figure of the little infant Jesus.

The pastor walked up to the boy and inquired, "Where did you get Him, my fine friend?"

The little boy replied, "I got Him from the church."

"And why did you take Him?"

The boy answered, "Well, about a week before Christmas I prayed to the little Lord Jesus and I told Him if He would bring me a red wagon for Christmas, I would give Him a ride around the block in it."

Since Christ's birth was a fulfillment of God's promise to His people, Christmas is a great time to make sure we are following through on our promises, too.

Sustain me according to your promise . . .

Psalm 119:116a

Lord, help me...
follow through on my promises!

He was a kind, decent, mostly good man, generous to his family, upright in his dealings with other men, but he just didn't believe all that incarnation stuff which the churches proclaim at Christmastime. It just did not make sense and he was too honest to pretend otherwise.

He just couldn't swallow the Jesus story about God come to earth as a man. He told his wife, "I'm not going to church with you this Christmas Eve." He said he'd feel like a hypocrite, that he'd much rather stay at home, but that he would wait up for them. And so he stayed home while they went to the midnight service.

Shortly after the family drove away in the car, snow began to fall. He went to the window to watch the flurries getting heavier and heavier, and then went back to his fireside chair and began to read his newspaper. Minutes later he was startled by a thudding sound, then another, and then another. At first he thought someone must be throwing snowballs against his living room window. But when he went to the front door to investigate, he found a flock of birds huddled miserably in the snow. They'd been caught in the storm, and in a desperate search for shelter had tried to fly through his large living room window.

Well, he couldn't let the poor creatures lie there and freeze, so he thought about the barn where his children stabled their pony. That would provide a warm shelter if he could direct the birds to it.

Hurriedly, he put on a coat and boots and tramped through the deepening snow to the barn. He opened the door wide and turned on a light. But the birds did not come in. He figured food would entice them, so he hurried back to the house, fetched bread crumbs, and sprinkled them on the snow to make a trail to the yellow-lighted wide-open doorway of the stable. But to his dismay, the birds ignored the bread crumbs and continued to flop around helplessly in the snow.

He tried catching them, he tried shooing them into the barn by walking around them waving his arms. Instead, the birds scattered in every direction except into the warm lighted barn. And then he realized that they were afraid of him. He thought to himself, "To them I am a strange and terrifying creature. If only I could think of some way to let them know that they could trust me, that I'm not trying to hurt them but help them. But how?" Any move that he made tended to frighten them, confuse them. They just would not be led or shooed because they feared him.

"If only I could be a bird," he thought to himself, "and mingle with them and speak their language. Then I could show them the way to the safe warm barn. But I would have to be one of them so they could see, and hear, and understand."

At that moment the church bells began to ring. The sound reached his ears above the sounds of the wind, and he stood there listening to the bells, listening to the bells heralding the glad tidings of the Savior's birth, and he sank to his knees in the snow.

The Gift

> *"Which is greater: the gift, or the altar that makes the gift sacred?"*
>
> Matthew 23:19b

An African boy listened carefully as the teacher explained why it is that Christians give presents to each other on Christmas Day.

"The gift is an expression of our joy over the birth of Jesus and our friendship for each other," she said.

When Christmas Day came, the boy brought the teacher a beautiful sea shell. "Where did you ever find such a beautiful shell?" the teacher asked.

The youth told her such extraordinary shells could be found in only one spot—a bay some miles away.

"Why it's beautiful!" the teacher exclaimed. "But you shouldn't have walked all that way to bring me a gift."

His eyes brightening, the boy answered, "Long walk—part of gift."

Lord, help me...
give myself to God
who gave me You!

Prayers In a Wagon

Harold Kohn, in "The Tinsel and the Hay," tells this story.

It was the Christmas season and a meeting was held in a small church for the announced purpose of praying for a local family that was having a tough time of it. The family was large and they didn't have enough food or enough money to keep the place properly heated.

As the people of the church prayed, there was some noise at the door of the church. They looked up and the young son of one of the elders had come in and shut the door with a bit of clumsiness and noise.

As all the people were staring at him, he said, "My dad couldn't make it tonight to the prayer meeting so he sent his prayers in my wagon. Could you help me bring them in?"

His prayers consisted of a sack of potatoes, a quarter of beef, several bags of vegetables, flour, apples, and other assorted staples.

The prayer meeting was immediately adjourned.

O Lord my God, I called to you for help and you healed me. . .you removed my sackcloth and clothed me with joy.

Psalm 30:2, 11b

Lord, help me...
put my prayers into action.

Gifts That Count

How can we draw closer to Christ this Christmas? Here are a few suggestions: First, read the Christmas story every day this month. It's found in Matthew 1:18–2:12 and in Luke 2:1–20.

Second, give gifts from the heart. Don't buy a gift just because you "have" to. How sad if we let Christmas become more pressure-filled than pleasure-filled! How sad if the pace is more pervasive than His peace!

Make a list of those to whom you want to give gifts from the heart. Then set your imagination free! Give a night or two of baby-sitting, give several grocery-shopping or errand-running trips, make picture books for children from old magazines, bake a special treat, write a poem or a from-the-heart message.

Third, remember whose birthday it is. How do you give a gift to Jesus? How do you send it to Him? What does the King need?

We give a gift to Him by giving His love to others, by giving shelter to a homeless family, by finding a gift for a child whose parent is in prison, by taking food to an elderly neighbor, by inviting several families and/or singles to join us in caroling at a nursing home (early in the evening!), by asking someone to attend the church Christmas program, by giving time to someone who is disillusioned, discouraged, or depressed.

And it isn't always just the poor who need us. Remember that a lot of lonely people live in a lot of big houses. Maybe a well-to-do family needs your supportiveness while they endure a difficult time.

Just as money doesn't guarantee happiness, it also doesn't guarantee friendship. The most important, the most meaningful gifts are not necessarily those that come in the biggest boxes with the fanciest wrapping, but are those that come from your heart.

For God so loved the world that he gave his one and only Son...

John 3:16

Lord, help me...
as I give others my simple gifts, help me
remember that I give to them, but I give for Him!

Christmas Begins

"*Therefore go...*"

Matthew 28:19

When the song of the angels is silent,
When the star in the sky is gone,
When the Kings and Princes are home,
When the shepherds are again tending their sheep,
When the manger is darkened and still,
The work of Christmas begins...

> To find the lost,
> To heal the broken,
> To feed the hungry,
> To rebuild the nations,
> To bring peace among people,
> To befriend the lonely,
> To release the prisoner,
> To make music in the heart.

Lord, help me...
accomplish the real work of Christmas—
all through the year!

Moving Too Fast

Did you hear about this lady? In the rush of last-minute Christmas shopping, a woman bought a box of 50 identical greeting cards. Without bothering to read the verse, she hastily signed and addressed all but one of them. Several days after they had been mailed, she came across the one card which hadn't been sent.

She was startled to read, "This card is just to say… a little gift is on the way."

My sheep listen to my voice; I know them, and they follow me.

John 10:27

Lord, help me…
if it deserves my full attention—
how much have I given you today?

Follow That Light

For Christmas a few years ago, Robyn Stevens bought her father a flashlight—a small, garden-variety, three-cell, waterproof flashlight. Several weeks after Christmas, January 16, 1993, her father and two other men were 25 miles from shore in the Gulf of Main, bringing the tugboat Harkness in from a construction job. Halfway home the Harkness and its crew found themselves sailing straight into a winter storm, with violent winds and temperatures of -60 degrees.

About 6:00 p.m., the captain realized that the boat was taking on water fast. The decks were sheer ice, the tug was pitching violently and they couldn't see anything because of sea smoke, six feet of impenetrable condensation above the ocean, caused by the temperature difference between ocean and air. Their message to the Coast Guard station was concise: "We're going down." When they realized they had to abandon ship, they made one last radio transmission. "The water is up to our chests in the wheelhouse. We're going into the water."

Three lobstermen heard their cry for help on the radio, left their families, and set out to find the sinking tugboat. As the rescue boat plowed through eight-foot waves, they had little hope of finding Robyn's father and his two friends. But after a little while, one of them saw a thin beam of light piercing the sea smoke.

Rick shouted to the captain, "Look over there. Follow that light." As they did, they found three half-dead men in the icy water, their arms hooked together and their arms frozen to a ladder that had come loose from the Harkness when it went down.

The men had long since lost their ability to hold on to anything. But the freezing cold had done the men a favor. Frozen to the back of one of Robyn's father's gloves was a small, garden-variety, three-cell waterproof flashlight. And the beam of that flashlight was pointing straight up to the sky. It saved their lives!

Jesus came down at Christmas to be that thin beam of light that shines through the darkness of despair, the winds of worry, the cold of confusion, and the sea smoke of sickness and sorrow. And since we are spiritually connected to Jesus, that thin beam of light shines through us, too.

Like the flashlight Robyn gave to her father, our flashlight is empowered by three cells: faith, hope, and love. Through the fog of fear and the darkness of doubt, may our friends and family see that thin beam of light in us this holiday season.

Lord, help me...
be willing to go through the storms of life with a
garden-variety flashlight as long as You supply the batteries!

Christmas Is...

...they rejoice before you as people rejoice at the harvest...

Isaiah 9:3a

Christmas is celebration, and celebration is instinct in the heart. With gift and feast, with scarlet ribbon and fresh green bough, with merriment and the sound of music, we commend the day—an oasis in the long, long landscape of the commonplace. Through how many centuries, through how many threatening circumstances, has Christmas been celebrated since the cry came ringing down the ages, "Fear not; for behold, I bring you good tidings of great joy, which shall be to all people. For unto you is born this day in the city of David a Savior, who is Christ, the Lord."

Faith and hope and love, which cannot be bought or sold or bartered but only given away, are the wellsprings, firm and deep, of Christmas celebration. These are the gifts without price, the ornaments incapable of imitation, discovered only within oneself and therefore unique. They are not always easy to come by; but they are in unlimited supply, ever in the province of all.

This Christmas, mend a quarrel. Seek out a forgotten friend. Dismiss suspicion and replace it with trust. Write a love letter. Share some treasure. Give a soft answer. Encourage youth. Manifest your loyalty in word and deed. Keep a promise. Find the time.

Forego a grudge. Forgive an enemy. Listen. Apologize if you were wrong. Try to understand. Forsake envy. Examine your demands on others. Think first of someone else. Appreciate. Be kind; be gentle. Laugh a little. Laugh a little more. Deserve confidence. Take up arms against malice.

Christmas is a celebration, but no celebration compares with the realization of the true meaning of Christmas—with the sudden stirring of the heart that has extended itself toward the core of life. Then, only then, is it possible to grasp the significance of that first Christmas; to savor in the inward ear the wild, sweet music of the Angel Choir; to envision the star-struck sky, and glimpse, behind the eyelids, the ray of light that fell on a darkened path and changed the world.

Lord, help me...
stay in Your loving care at Christmas and
throughout the coming year.

About the Authors

John M. Palmer is recognized as a highly effective communicator and motivator. Since 1985, he has served as the charismatic and much-admired senior pastor of First Assembly of God Church in Des Moines, Iowa.

Under his inspiring leadership, weekend worship attendance averages nearly 3,000. The congregation experiences continuing growth and is known for its community involvement and outreach.

He has authored a book on spiritual gifts, contributed chapters to several book collections, and written articles for leading Christian publications.

He serves on many national as well as community boards, and meets regularly with many of Des Moines' pastors for prayer and mutual encouragement.

A graduate of Central Bible College in Springfield, Missouri, John M. Palmer was named 1998 Alumnus of the Year.

Linda Delbridge, Ph.D., earned her B.A. at Buena Vista University and her graduate degrees from Iowa State University. She has taught middle school through college-level language arts, k-12 talented-and-gifted, and graduate education courses, and has held educational research positions. She has over 100 publications to her credit, and has received numerous awards and recognitions.

Permissions & Acknowledgements

January

Introduction: Palmer, John M.
There's a Way: Palmer, John M.
The Courage to Continue: Palmer, John M.
Winners: Palmer, John M.
Strategic Thinking: "Ten Guidelines" McDonough, Reginald.
Nose Prints: Palmer, John M.
A Time for Reflection: Palmer, John M.

February

Introduction: Palmer, John M.
Love: "You are Sixteen." The Sound of Music. Music and words by Rogers, Richard and Oscar Hammerstein, 1959.
Reach Up: Palmer, John M.
The Perfect Cure: Palmer, John M.

March

Introduction: Delbridge, Linda, Ph.D.
No News Is Good News: Palmer, John M.
Better Now than Later!: Palmer, John M.
Anticipating with Confidence: Palmer, John M.
The Touch of Love: Rogers, Sherman.
The Move Is On: Palmer, John M.
Seatbelts and Supplications: Palmer, John M.

April

Introduction: Palmer, John M.
Only Then Could He Plant: Delbridge, Linda, Ph.D.
Coming Full Circle: Palmer, John M.
A Lesson From the Links: Palmer, John M.
Getting Ready: Palmer, John M.
Priorities: Palmer, John M.

May

Introduction: Palmer, John M.
A Grad and Her Dad: Palmer, John M.
Small—But Mighty: Ratz, Calvin.
Leading by Example: Elliot, Elisabeth, "The Mark of a Man," Fleming H. Revell Co.,
a division of Baker Book House, 1981.
I Love Storms: Palmer, John M.
The Power of a Seed: Harvey, Paul.
Mom is "Wow": McDermott, Jacqueline; Palmer, John M.
Slow Me Down, Lord: Crane, Orin.
Happy Pappy: Palmer, John M.
A Time for Reflection: Montapert, Alfred.

June

Introduction: Palmer, John M.
Teammates: Palmer, John M.
Picking Each Other Up: Palmer, John M.
Walt: Hendricks, Howard and William Hendricks, Moody Press.
Umpiring for Jesus: Palmer, John M.

July

Introduction: Palmer, John M.
One Step at a Time: Palmer, John M.
Go 4 It!: Palmer, John M.
Paying to Volunteer: Palmer, John M.

August

Introduction: Palmer, John M.
When Tin Cans Taste Good: Pulpit Helps from Soul's Harvest.
He Gave a Warm Blanket: Pulpit Helps from Soul's Harvest.
God Did It With a Crayon: Dunham, Nan.
Finally Forty: Palmer, John M.

September

Introduction: Palmer, John M.
All About Healing: Delbridge, Linda, Ph.D.
From the "Money" Section: Dorfman, Dan; Palmer, John M.
You Can Make It: Palmer, John M.

October

Introduction: Palmer, John M.
Better Not to Know: Schuller, Robert H., Ph.D.
Sow Seeds, Reap Fruit: Pulpit Helps from Soul's Harvest.
Sparky Was a Loser: Harvey, Paul.

November

Power of a Grateful Heart: Beecher, Henry Ward.
Unseen Harvest: Palmer, John M.
The Unsung Heroes: Friedman, Tom.
Rejoice Always: Galloway, Dale, "Rebuild Your Life," 800-420-2048.

December

Introduction: Palmer, John M.
Truths From the Turnpike: Palmer, John M.
The Gift: reprinted with permission from "The Guideposts Christmas Treasury,"
Guideposts, Carmel, New York 10512, 1972.
Prayers in a Wagon: Kohn, Harold.
Gifts that Count: Palmer, John M.
Christmas Begins: Parables, Etc.
Follow That Light: Palmer, John M.

Notes